THE
Stompbox

by
Art Thompson

MF Miller Freeman Books

Published by Miller Freeman Books, 600 Harrison Street, San Francisco, CA 94107
Publishers of *Guitar Player*, *Bass Player* and *Keyboard* magazines
Miller Freeman, Inc. is a United News and Media Company

 Miller Freeman
A United News & Media publication

Distributed to the book trade in the U.S. and Canada by Publishers Group West,
P.O. Box 8843, Emeryville, CA 94662

Distributed to the music trade in the U.S. and Canada by Hal Leonard Publishing,
P.O. Box 13819, Milwaukee, WI 53213

ISBN 0-87930-479-0

Cover Design: Ark Stein, The Visual Group
Cover Photo of Jimi Hendrix: Joseph Sia
Cover Photos of Stompboxes: Paul Haggard

Text Design: Gestalt Graphics

Printed in the United States of America
97 98 99 00   5 4 3 2 1

This book is dedicated
to my wife Christine
for her patience and understanding,
and to the memory
of my father,
who took the time to show me
how things worked.

Thanks to:

Bruce Barr (Sound Barrier Music, Chattanooga, Tennessee), Steve Bischer, Jack Brossart, Terry Buddingh, Mitch Colby, Ritchie Fliegler, Paul Haggard, Robert Hamilton (Univibe Music, Oakland, California), John Hawkins, George Janis (Janis Music, Manteca, California), Gordon Kennedy, John Lomas, Steve Macari, Kevin Macy, Jerry McPhereson, Mark Sampson, James Santiago, Steve Soest, Dave Stein (The Starving Musician, Santa Clara, California), Ralph Tolson (High Tech Audio, San Francisco, California), George Tripps, Randy Wright, and *Guitar Player* magazine

ConTents

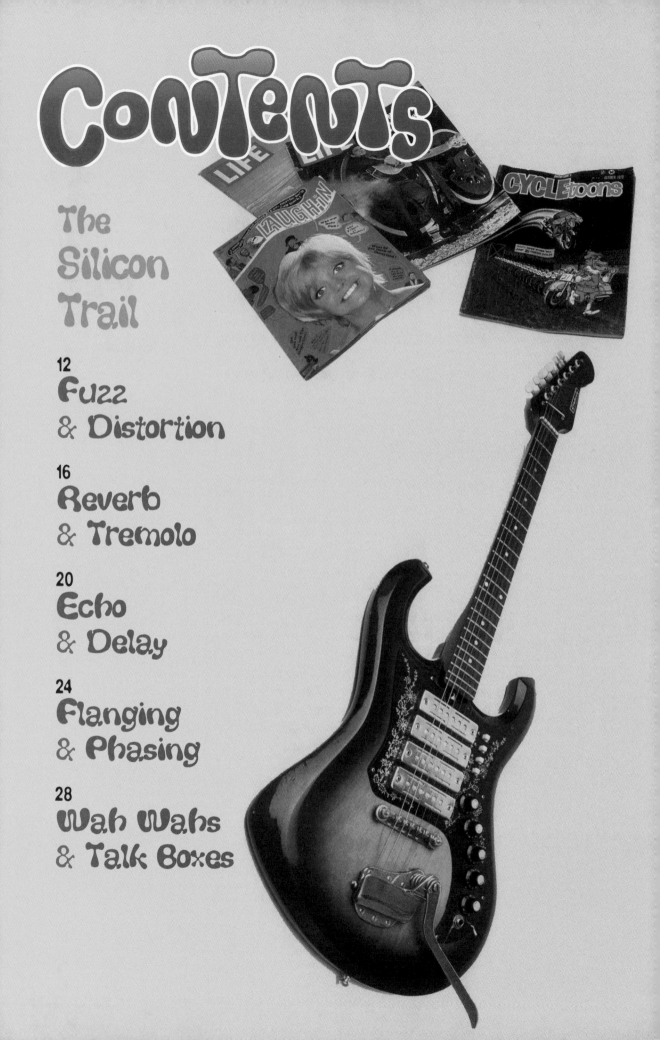

The Silicon Trail

12
Fuzz
& Distortion

16
Reverb
& Tremolo

20
Echo
& Delay

24
Flanging
& Phasing

28
Wah Wahs
& Talk Boxes

The Makers

36
ADA

42
Arbiter

46
Dan Armstrong

50
DOD

56
Electro-Harmonix

64
Fender

68
Foxx

74
Ibanez

84
Maestro

92
Roger Mayer

96
Morley

102
Mosrite

106
MXR

112
Mu-Tron Musitronics

120
Pro Co

128
Roland /Boss

134
Seamoon

136
Sola Colorsound

138
Tube Works

142
Tychobrahe

146
Univox

152
Vox

INTRODUCTION

The human need for self-expression is boundless, and in a crowded and indifferent world, it's usually the loudest and most outrageous who get noticed first. In pop music, the stompboxes and pedals that surfaced in the wake of the mid-'60s guitar mania opened the floodgates of sonic expression.

The revolution had its roots in the invention of the transistor in 1948 by Bell Laboratories physicists William Shockley, Walter Brattain and John Bardeen. The impact of solid-state technology on the era's music was immense. By the early '50s, transistors had found their way into consumer audio gear, and the music instrument industry was hot on the trail. Transistors were cheaper and more reliable than vacuum tubes, but their real beauty was their small size and low power requirements, which allowed an almost endless variety of tone-shaping circuits to be conveniently inserted between guitar and amplifier. Electronic concepts such as clipping, filtering, phase shifting, flanging, and amplitude and frequency modulation (tremolo and vibrato) predated transistors, but solid-state technology made it possible to bring these sound shapers to the market in a practical and low-cost form.

Most of the mid-century electronics advances would likely have been squandered on the home organ had it not been for the electric guitar craze that was ignited by the British Invasion. An estimated 73 million peo-

with *Maestro* Fuzz-Tone

ple in 23,240,000 homes across America tuned in on February 9, 1964, to watch the Beatles perform on the Ed Sullivan Show in New York City. When the lights came back on that night, a lot of people saw a 6-string in their future.

By the end of the '60s, effects had become an indispensable part of pop music. Jeff Beck's fuzz-wah freakouts on *Truth*, the buzz-saw riffs of the Rolling Stones' "(I Can't Get No) Satisfaction" and Count Five's "Psychotic Reaction," and Jimi Hendrix's epochal *Are You Experienced?*, *Axis: Bold as Love*, and *Electric Ladyland* were bold testaments to the power of silicon.

Stompbox builders catered to the lust for sonic outrage with an enormous variety of sound modification devices, many of which are as important today as they were in the peace-and-love era. Some of the companies that started in garages and basements became signal-processing superstars, while others faded into oblivion. One thing they all had in common, though, was a sense of adventure and a willingness to risk everything in pursuit of tone. This book is dedicated to the people who made stompboxes happen. Their stories are presented as they were told.

FUZZ & DISTORTION

Compared with luthiers and amp builders, stompbox makers have always been on guitar gear's lunatic fringe, getting about the same degree of peer respect as aboriginal medicine men do from brain surgeons. The early effects scene, especially, was the domain of techs and tinkerers, most of whom labored in semi-obscurity. Sometimes they stumbled into the business accidentally. Such was the case with Glen Snotty, a Nashville studio engineer who made a huge impact on guitar sound while attempting to solve a studio inconvenience.

The story is told by Harold Bradley, president of Nashville's Local 257 of the American Federation of Musicians and a longtime session guitarist. In 1951, Harold and his brother Owen built Nashville's famed Quonset Hut recording studio, a veritable skunk works for country stars such as Patsy Cline, Loretta Lynn, Brenda Lee, and Conway Twitty. According to Harold, session guitarist Grady Martin, playing a Danelectro short-scale bass, was getting ready to lay down a solo for Marty Robbins' 1961 hit "Don't Worry" when a channel in the studio's tube-powered mixing board began distorting. Normally the session would have stopped until a repair was made, but this time someone liked the sound and Grady went with it. Harold Bradley says the result was Nashville's first recorded fuzz solo.

'60s Sam Ash Fuzz.

Guyatone tube-powered distorter.

Buzz galore: the Clark fuzz.

Jordan's cool-sounding Boss Tone plugged right into your guitar.

This could have been just another studio oddity, but Bradley contends that when other artists heard Grady's solo on the finished song, they too wanted to use the studio's "magic" fuzz effect. But by this time the mixing board had been repaired and the sound was gone. Some clients didn't buy this explanation, however, grumbling that the Bradleys were hoarding the effect for their own artists. Weary of the complaints, Snotty cooked up a transistorized circuit that approximated the sound he'd heard from the board's buzzing channel, and the box quickly became a hot Nashville item.

Harold says Glen later gave the circuit to someone from Gibson, which subsequently introduced a distortion box called the Maestro Fuzz-Tone. L.A. session king Tommy Tedesco recalled using the brown, wedge-shaped Maestro on the theme to Green Acres, which first aired in '65: "I think I was the original guy with a Fuzz-Tone in California when they first came out. It was the only one available at the time," Tommy told *Guitar Player* magazine in 1992.

MPC Electra guitars featured plug-in modules that offered effects like fuzz, phase shifter, treble/bass expander, tank tone, overdrive, triggered filter, auto wah, tube sound, octave box, flanger, and the frog nose headphone amp.

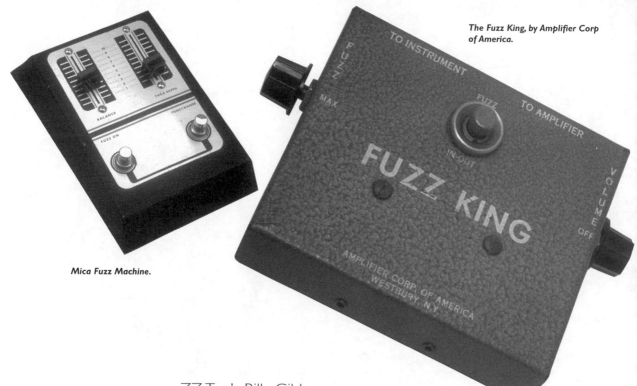

The Fuzz King, by Amplifier Corp of America.

Mica Fuzz Machine.

ZZ Top's Billy Gibbons says the Fuzz-Tone is the first effects box he ever heard: "Oh, man, that's as contraptionalized a piece as one might want to tackle. Every one I've heard produces a slightly different sound. There's a Fender Jaguar I've had since 1967 that contains the guts of a Maestro that had been modified by a guy in Texas. Somehow it was wired through a glass-dial meter; I don't remember what it measured, but it sure sounded great!"

The Doors' Robbie Krieger and Yes's Steve Howe were Maestro Fuzz-Tone users, as was Keith Richards, who helped bring fuzz to the world's attention with his Maestro-ized riff in '65's "(I Can't Get No) Satisfaction."

Glen Snotty's creation may have led to big-company involvement with a fuzz effect, but guitarists had been using distortion tricks since the '50s. Roy Buchanan spoke of slicing his speakers to get fuzz, and there's the famous story of the Rock 'N Trio's Paul Burlison, who accidentally dropped his amp before a session, loosening an output tube to the point that it no longer functioned in the circuit. He liked the resulting buzz so much that he used it on his 1956 classic, "Train Kept A-Rollin" and "Honey Hush."

Nashville and Memphis studio legend Reggie Young echoes this story with his own recollections of intentionally removing an output tube or feeding the speaker output of one amp into the input of another to

drive it into distortion. He also recalls owning a Canadian-made tube-powered device called a Herzog that was designed to overdrive the front end of a guitar amp. "It was a little smaller than a Fender amp head," Young says, "and so noisy that I had to use it with a volume pedal to keep the hiss down until I played."

When it was discovered that Hank Garland's amp would emit a whisper-level distorted tone when placed on standby, the engineer (probably Glen Snotty) sent the signal direct to the board and used it on a session for 17-year-old Ann-Margret's first record, in '58 or '59.

Another Nashville legend, Chet Atkins, has said his first use of overdrive predates the "Don't Worry" session: "I used that years and years ago—back in the '50s. I had a guy build me one. It was a little transistorized preamp, right after transistors came out. It was about the size of a snuffbox." Heavy metal pioneer Ritchie Blackmore says a band called the Rip Chords was the first to record a fuzzbox solo, in 1957, and he credits guitarist Bernie Watson with recording England's first fuzz solo, on Screaming Lord Sutch's 1960 "Jack the Ripper."

Historical claims notwithstanding, the words of grunge frontiersman Link Wray (in a 1993 Guitar Player story) best embody the spirit of the distortion quest: "I had a Premier amplifier with a big speaker on the bottom and two tweeters on each amp. It was a crossover head. I got me a pen and started punching holes in the speakers. [Link's brother] Ray said, 'You're just screwin' with your amplifier.' I said, 'Who cares as long as we get a fuckin' sound, man!'"

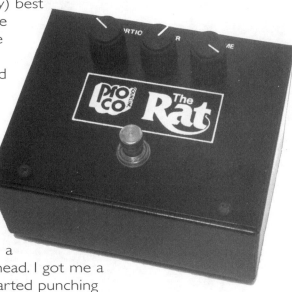

ProCo's Rat

ReVerb & TREMOLO

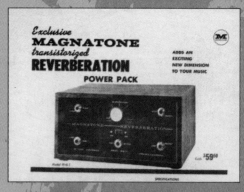

Early '60s Magnatone stand-alone reverb.

Humans have known the power of reverb ever since they first noticed how countless small echoes could be created by grunting inside a large, enclosed area—probably a cave. Medieval cathedrals exploited the concept, and early studio builders brought it into the 20th century by placing a speaker at one end of a hard-surfaced room and a microphone at the other. Signals pumped into the speaker were picked up by the mike as a conglomeration of short, ricocheting echoes, or reverb. Cool sounding, but hardly portable. In a 1984 Guitar Player interview, Duane Eddy described a cumbersome device used on his early hits such as "Rebel-'Rouser" and "Movin' 'N' Groovin'": "The studio didn't have an echo chamber, so they bought an empty water tank and put a speaker in one end and a mike in the other. There was no room inside the studio for this big 500-gallon iron tank, so they set it outside. We used to have to chase the birds off of it sometimes. We also had to stop recording if a siren went by or a plane flew over, because it picked up everything."

Hidden inside little David's miniature Leslie cabinet was a solid-state vibrato circuit.

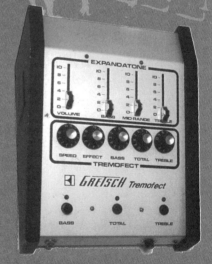

The super tweakable Gretsch Tremofect with Expandatone EQ.

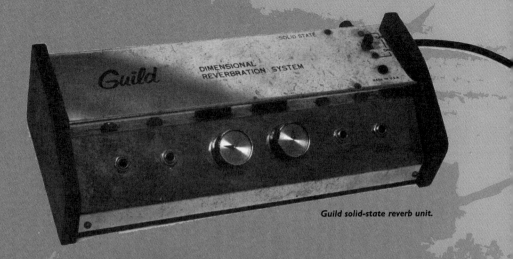

Guild solid-state reverb unit.

Clusters of very short echoes could be created by putting a signal into a transducer that was coupled mechanically to one end of a long spring, with another transducer attached to the other end. The driving transducer converted electrical energy into mechanical energy, while the opposite conversion took place at the other end. As the spring rippled, exponential numbers of additional "reflections" were added. Toss in some driver-and-recovery circuitry and a power amp and speakers, and the result was electro-mechanical reverb.

Hammond Organ was one of the earliest spring reverb producers, and their license of the circuit to Fender led to the model 6G-15 Reverb Unit. Introduced in 1961, this all-tube stand-alone device set the standard for guitar reverb, and would become one of Fender's most important contributions to the effects scene.

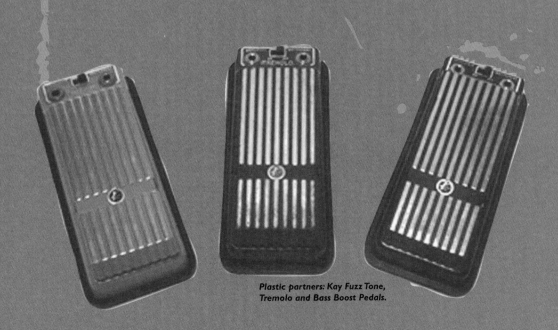

Plastic partners: Kay Fuzz Tone, Tremolo and Bass Boost Pedals.

Emerging in the late '40s, tremolo and vibrato were among the first available guitar sound modifiers, and while both are examples of modulated effects, they differ distinctly. Tremolo refers to a cyclical amplitude

change—like repeatedly turning your guitar volume control up and down—while vibrato refers to cyclical pitch fluctuations. DeArmond's Tremolo Control (available in both pedal and stand-alone versions) contained an electric-motor-driven eccentric wheel that rocked a little tube of mercury, opening and closing the circuit. Later tremolo designs, such as the one Leo Fender called "vibrato," used more refined circuitry in which (in the final version that Leo settled on) a low-frequency oscillator (LFO) pulsed a light source directed at a photo resistor. As the light got brighter, the photo resistor allowed more

signal to pass. As it dimmed, resistance increased, lowering the signal level. Placed in-between the preamp and the output stage of an amplifier, the circuit makes volume fluctuate at a rate set by the LFO.

True vibrato can be an ugly effect, but that didn't stop some companies from expending lots of effort per-fecting it. Gibson got serious about vibrato in 1956 with the model GA-VI Electronic Vibrato unit and the GA89S guitar amp, which featured an all-tube pitch-shift oscillator and stereo power amps. Magnatone fol-lowed in the early '60s with their vibrato-equipped 480 and 280 model combos. "I used a reworked Magnatone on 'Rebel-'Rouser,'" recalled Duane Eddy, "and then I had one custom-built with a new tremolo circuit and everything. I com-pared it to everything that came around, and noth-ing could match it."

Strange but true: Fender's spacy Dimension IV reverb/vibrato unit featured a Morley-made memory system that involved an oil-filled can and an electric motor.

ECHO & DELAY

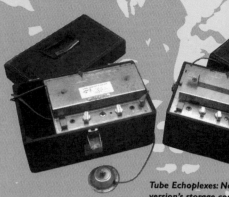

Tube Echoplexes: Note the earlier version's storage compartment.

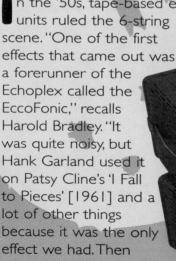

The Butts-built EchoSonic featured onboard tape echo. Scotty Moore used this amp on most of Elvis Presley's late Sun and early RCA singles.

Recording a signal onto tape and then retrieving it a split second later via the playback head was one of the earliest ways of creating artificial echo. Chet Atkins remembered using a Magnacorder tape recorder to get a slow delay effect on "Blue Ocean Echo": "I ran the machine at 7-1/2 inches per second and moved the playback head a certain distance so it would echo at the tempo I wanted."

In the '50s, tape-based echo units ruled the 6-string scene. "One of the first effects that came out was a forerunner of the Echoplex called the EccoFonic," recalls Harold Bradley. "It was quite noisy, but Hank Garland used it on Patsy Cline's 'I Fall to Pieces' [1961] and a lot of other things because it was the only effect we had. Then came the Echoplex, and I liked that better than anything."

Reggie Young recalls, "In the mid '50s, I was playing the Turf Club in Cairo, Illinois, with a Western swing band. There was a music store in town owned by a guy named Ray Butts. Ray had made some amplifiers with built-in tape echoes for Chet Atkins and Scotty Moore, and there was one in that store. I walked in one day and tried it, and it freaked me right out. I thought, 'Man alive, this is great!' Later, when I moved to Nashville, Ray was working in

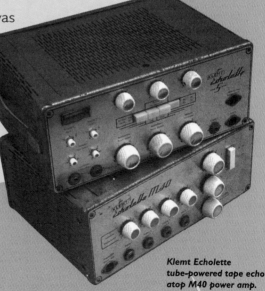

Klemt Echolette tube-powered tape echo atop M40 power amp.

20

The Italian-made Binson Echorec stored sounds via magnetic disk.

Variations on the analog delay theme.

the electronics department at RCA. I brought him an Echoplex that was really noisy, and he fixed it for me. He told me he designed the Echoplex—Ray was definitely way ahead of his time."

In the early '50s, Butts (who was also a radio repairman) was asked by a friend to build a device that could simulate the echo on Les Paul's recordings. Ray created a primitive tape loop by tying a knot in the recording wire of an old wire-type recorder; he then installed the unit in a Gibson amp. The idea worked, sort of. Butts next experimented with loops made of copper tubing and paper-backed recording tape. When acetate recording tape was introduced, Ray reworked the amp/echo unit to his satisfaction and sold it to his friend.

"I never made a separate

echo unit," Ray says. "There were a lot of bad amplifiers being made at that time, so I figured that if I built the echo into my own amp, then I could be sure it would sound the way I wanted. That's why I never offered it as an accessory."

Ray says he later borrowed back his friend's 25-watt amp for a trip to Nashville, where he demonstrated it to Chet Atkins. Chet promptly ordered one of the amps— now called the EchoSonic— and soon after, Scotty Moore, Carl Perkins, Roy Orbison, and Johnny Cash guitarist

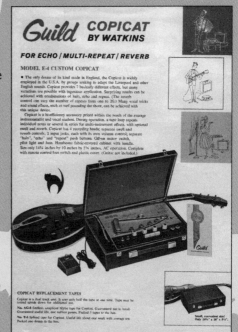

Circa '65 Copicat ad.

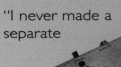

Electro-Harmonix Memory Man analog delays.

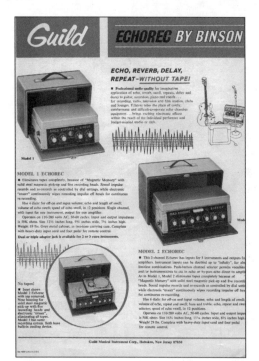

Guild ECHOREC BY BINSON

ECHO, REVERB, DELAY, REPEAT—WITHOUT TAPE!

■ Professional audio quality for imaginative application of echo, reverb, swell, repeats, delay and decay to guitar, accordion, piano and vocals . . . for recording, radio, television and film studios, clubs and lounges. Echorec takes the place of costly, cumbersome and difficult-to-operate echo chamber equipment . . . brings exciting electronic effects within the reach of the individual performer and budget-minded studio or club.

MODEL 1 ECHOREC

■ Eliminates tapes completely, because of "Magnetic Memory" with solid steel magnetic pick-up and five recording heads. Sound impulse records and re-records as controlled by dial settings, while electronic "eraser" continuously wipes recording impulse off heads for continuous re-recording.

Has 4 dials: for off-on and input volume; echo and length of swell; volume of echo swell; speed of echo swell; in 12 positions. Single channel, with input for one instrument, output for one amplifier.

Operates on 110-280 volts AC, 50-60 cycles. Input and output impedance is 50K ohms. Size 12½ inches long, 9½ inches wide, 7½ inches high. Weight 19 lbs. Grey metal cabinet, in two-tone carrying case. Complete with heavy-duty input card and foot pedal for remote control.

Dual or triple adapter jack is available for 2 or 3 extra instruments.

MODEL 2 ECHOREC

■ This 3-channel Echorec has inputs for 3 instruments and outputs for 3 amplifiers. Instrument inputs can be doubled up to "intensify", for six limitless combinations. Push-button channel selector permits vocalists and/or instrumentalists to cut in echo or by-pass echo direct to amplifier. As in Model 1, Model 2 eliminates tapes completely because of "Magnetic Memory" with solid steel magnetic pick-up and five recording heads. Sound impulse records and re-records as controlled by dial settings while electronic "eraser" continuously wipes recording impulse off heads for continuous re-recording.

Has 6 dials: for off-on and input volume; echo and length of swell; volume of echo, repeat and swell; bass and treble; echo, repeat and swell selector; speed of echo swell, in 12 positions.

Operates on 110-280 volts AC, 50-60 cycles. Input and output impedance is 50K ohms. Size 16½ inches long, 11¼ inches wide, 8½ inches high. Weight 29 lbs. Complete with heavy-duty input card and four pedal for remote control.

No tapes!

■ Inset shows Model 2 Echorec with top removed. Note housing for solid steel magnetic pick-up with five recording heads and electronic "eraser", eliminating all tapes. Model 1 has same recording system. Both have built-in cooling device.

Guild Musical Instrument Corp., Hoboken, New Jersey 07030

1965 Echorec promo.

Guild distributed the British-made Watkins Custom Copicat.

Luther Perkins bought them. Moore used the EchoSonic on most of Elvis's late Sun and early RCA singles. "I had the third one built," Moore recalled. "It had a tape, more like a slap-back effect—not the Echoplex we know of now with a repeater—but it just gave a little boost to the sound. It was awful good if you missed a note. It wouldn't come out so bad."

"Les Paul obtained echo by feeding his tape recorder's output back into the input," Ray Butts notes. "But I came up with the idea of an echo that didn't involve a tape recorder. When Les came to Nashville in '55 or '56, Chet Atkins already had one of my amplifiers and had played it on the Opry. Chet told me later that when Les appeared on the Opry, he looked at the amplifier and said, 'That's impossible—it can't be done.' You see, if you just use feedback to create echo, you can't really make the slapback effect. But you could get a slapback echo with my amplifier. It would make just a single repeat or a series, and you could vary the balance between the echo and the direct sound.

"There was another tape echo unit called the EccoFonic [distributed by Fender in the late '50s]. I had my attorney contact them because it was an infringement on my EchoSonic name. The owner of the company offered to buy my patent rights for $5,000. I didn't take him up on it, but I probably should have, because I never built any more of them.

"Later, a company called Market Electronics started making a tape echo called the Echoplex. I went to the factory in Cleveland, Ohio, and met with the owner, Bob Hunter. I showed him a copy

The EchoSonic's control panel

of my patent, and he didn't dispute that the Echoplex was an infringement on it. He first tried to get me to serve as a distributor, then he gave me a couple of units and promised me $500 a month. I got paid once or twice, but I didn't push the issue after that. He was in bad health, so I just let it go."

The Echoplex was later made by Chicago-based Harris-Teller and distributed by Maestro, and in the late '60s and early '70s various tapeless echo systems employing magnetic disks or electrostatic fluids (as in Tel-Ray's Ad-N-Echo) were introduced by a number of companies. Contenders included Fender (Echo-Reverb, Variable Echo Reverb, Soundette), Morley (Echo Volume, Echo Chorus Vibrato, Delay Echo Reverb, Electrostatic Delay Line), Thomas Organ, and Binson (Echorec). But the mid-'70s advent of solid-state "bucket brigade" technology offered the most promising alterna-

tive to tape for stage and studio echo. In a bucket-brigade circuit, a series of capacitors, or "buckets," delays the signal by passing an electron charge from bucket to bucket at an externally variable rate. Simpler and more reliable than its tape-based counterpart, this new type of echo, called analog delay, was first used in such stompboxes as the Electro-Harmonix Memory Man and MXR Analog Delay.

Rear view of Scotty Moore's EchoSonic.

flanging & PHASING

Analog delay could also produce effects such as flanging and chorusing that were difficult or impossible with tape. Bucket-brigade technology opened the door to solid-state flanging, an effect originally created using two tape recorders. As the machines played identical tracks, one was slowed by dragging a finger against the tape-reel flange to create delayed signals. When the signals were combined, the resulting peaks and notches in the frequency spectrum produced the effect's signature swooshing sound.

In the early days, the terms flanging and phase-shifting were sometimes used interchangeably. John Lennon reportedly referred to every effect used by producer George Martin as "flanging." Martin says Lennon coined the term.

It's hard to say who discovered flanging, but fingers point to Les Paul. For his 1945 recording "Mamie's Boogie," Les used two disk recorders—one equipped with variable speed control—to create the effect. Les explains, "I didn't do it on tape. You take two disks and start them out the same. I had one with a sync motor, which is 60 cycles sync, and the other was on an inductor motor, where I could change the speed with a Variac. I

Electro-Harmonix Bad Stone and Small Stone phase shifters and Small Clone chorus.

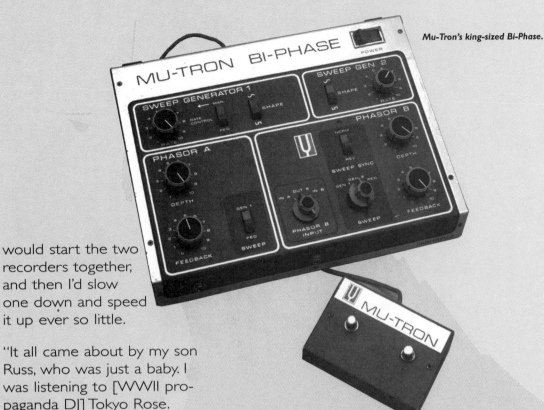

Mu-Tron's king-sized Bi-Phase.

would start the two recorders together, and then I'd slow one down and speed it up ever so little.

"It all came about by my son Russ, who was just a baby. I was listening to [WWII propaganda DJ] Tokyo Rose. She's playing one of my songs, but my kid doesn't know it's dad, so he moves the dial to a station coming from Berlin or someplace. I saw that he was intrigued by the sound being out of phase, and it intrigued me too. I wondered if it would intrigue other people the same way."

In the mid '70s, ADA founder David Tarnowsky developed a bucket-brigade flanging circuit for a Northern California effects company called Seamoon. Tarnowsky's design led directly to the famous ADA Flanger—one of the most radical effects of its day. Other well-known AC-powered flangers of this period included the Electro-Harmonix Electric Mistress, the MXR Flanger and the Tychobrahe Pedal Flanger.

Ludwig's circa-'70 Phase II.

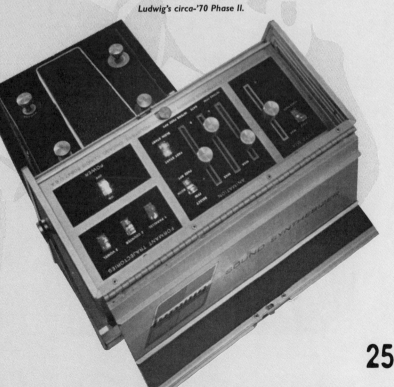

Chorusing, a close cousin to flanging, is the blurry, swirling effect that occurs when a sound moves slowly in and out of pitch. The first chorusing device was the Leslie rotating organ speaker, which relied on the Doppler effect. Electronic chorus units mimic Doppler pitch-bending by slowly increasing and decreasing a sine wave's pitch and then recombining the altered sound with the straight signal.

Electronic chorusing was introduced by Roland in 1976 in the CE-1 Chorus Ensemble, but it probably found its way on to more records via Roland's JC-120 Jazz Chorus amp, which featured built-in stereo chorus. The JC-120 spawned copies from nearly every major amp manufacturer, and even today, chorus likely trails only reverb in popularity for built-in amp effects. Early chorus-pedal offerings include Electro-Harmonix's Stereo Memory Man with Chorus,

MXR Flangers

Three ways to phase.

DOD's Stereo Chorus 565 and 565-A, MXR's Stereo Chorus, Ibanez's CS-505 Stereo Chorus, and the Boss CE-2.

The psychedelic swirl of phase-shifting is rooted in a circuit originally developed for notching out noise in radio transmissions, but '50s inventors exploited the concept in an attempt to simulate the liquid, wobbling sound of the Leslie. Phase shifters work by creating dips or notches at various frequencies, and then sweeping those notches up and down. In the early '70s, synth pioneer Tom Oberheim developed a compact, solid-state phaser for Maestro, the PS-1 Phase Shifter. The AC-powered device was a hit with musicians, and phase-shifting's popularity led to other early designs such as MXR's Phase 90, Roland's Phase Five, Electro-Harmonix's Small Stone, and ADA's Final Phase.

Kent Black Gold phase shifter.

27

Wah-Wahs & TALK BOXES

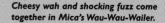
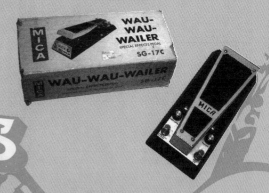

Rosac's Nu-Wa Nu-Fuzz was designed by Mosrite's Ed Sanner.

Next to the whammy bar, wah-wah ranks as one of the most profoundly expressive guitar effects ever created. Though Ampeg reportedly had experimented with a passive wah circuit as early as 1961, most wahs are based on an active circuit (a bandpass filter with a variable resonant frequency) developed in 1966 by Thomas Organ engineer Brad Plunkett.

Assigned the task of devising a circuit to replace the Vox Super Beatle amplifier's 3-position MRB (midrange boost) voicing switch with a less-costly potentiometer, Plunkett first modified an oscillator design suggested by fellow engineer Les Kushner. Brad then built the new circuit and began testing it with a guitar. "All of a sudden people came running in to see what was making this sound," Plunkett recalls. "They just freaked out." Thomas Organ reportedly considered a tremolo-arm method of actuating the pot, but instead fitted the wah circuitry into a volume pedal. The unit was introduced as the Clyde McCoy Wah-Wah pedal—Clyde being a popular trumpet player who had asked Vox for a device that could simulate the open-and-close mute effect.

Five flavors of Vox wah: (L-R) Fuzz Wah Volume, V-847, King Wah, Thomas Organ CryBaby, and Stereo Fuzz wah.

According to Vox engineer Dick Denney, these early wahs—which featured a picture of Clyde on the bottom plate—were initially made in the U.S. and England, and later in Italy. The introduction of the Vox CryBaby around 1968 came about because Thomas Organ/Vox and Britain's Vox/JMI both wanted to sell the wah-wah, but neither wanted the other to have the same pedal. Thomas Organ solved the problem by slapping "CryBaby" on the American version. The story goes that when Thomas Organ officials were trying to name the wah-wah, they asked one of their distributors to describe its sound. The response was, "It sounds like a baby crying."

Thomas Organ's wah pedal spawned copycats from practically every corner of the effects market, but one of the most original offshoots was the Musitronics Mu-Tron III, an envelope follower and voltage-controlled filter designed by former Guild consultant Mike Biegle. Introduced in 1972, the device produced wah-wah effects that responded to picking dynamics. When the strings were hit hard, the Mu-Tron sounded like a wah-wah with the pedal pressed down. Light picking produced the pedal-back sound.

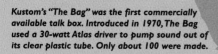

Kustom's "The Bag" was the first commercially available talk box. Introduced in 1970, The Bag used a 30-watt Atlas driver to pump sound out of its clear plastic tube. Only about 100 were made.

Beyond wah: Kent's nutty Bow-Wow Yoy-Yoy pedal.

Many effects aficionados still regard the Mu-Tron III as the coolest-sounding auto wah ever made. It too inspired numerous other envelope followers, including Electro-Harmonix's Doctor Q, Bass Balls, and Y Triggered Filter, and Seamoon's Funk Machine. One of the more original takes on non-pedal wah was the Electro-Harmonix Soul Kiss. About the size of a cigarette pack, the Soul Kiss featured an orally triggered sensor hard-wired to a cable. Opening and closing your mouth around the sensor produced the wah-wah effect.

The idea of using the mouth cavity as a sound-shaping filter dates back to 1939 and a device called the Sonavox, which used the output of an instrument amplifier to drive a transducer strapped to the player's neck. Operation was simple. As the transducer vibrated the vocal cords, the player could mouth sounds that made the instrument sound as if it were speaking. Steel guitar star Alvino Rey used the gizmo to create his famous talking-steel hits of the early '40s. He disconnected his amp's speakers so the entire output—probably a whopping 15 watts—drove the Sonavox.

Instead of a pedal, the Wah-Vol featured a pad that you twisted with your foot.

Japanese-made companion wah.

In the early '70s Nashville pedal steeler Pete Drake developed a gadget called the Talkin' Actuator. "You disconnect the speakers, and the sound goes through the driver into a plastic tube," Pete explained. "You put the tube in the side of your mouth and then form the words with your mouth as you play them." Drake used the effect on Roger Miller's "Lock Stock and Tear Drops" and Jim Reeves' "I've Enjoyed as Much of This as I Can Stand," and he later turned Peter Frampton on to the device.

According to Buddy Emmons, a pedal steel experimenter named Bill West improved on Drake's creation by fitting it with a horn driver that could withstand higher power. It was likely West who introduced the effect to Joe Walsh.

Japanese Surf, Hurricane and Wah pedal.

Southern California's Kustom company produced the world's first commercial talk box. Called The Bag, it consisted of a 30-watt Atlas driver inside a padded, cloth-covered bag that was slung over the shoulder. A switch on the side of the bag allowed the player to send the entire amplifier output into the Bag's driver, which was attached to a length of plastic tubing.

Mica Wau Wau Machine.

31

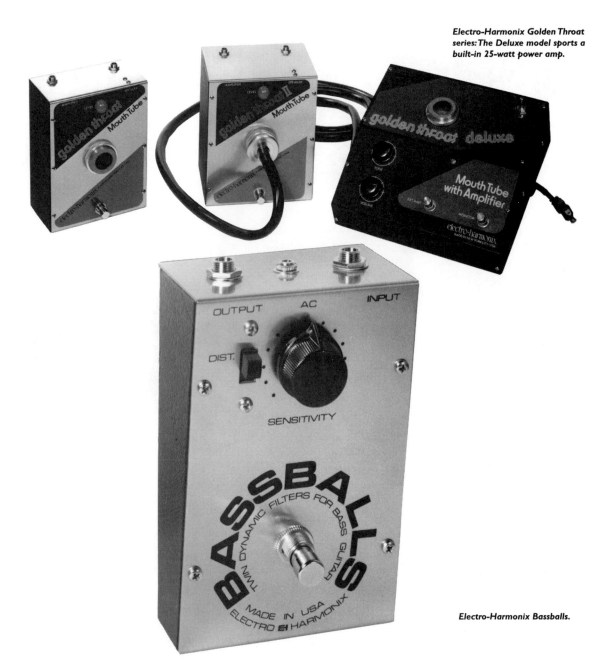

Electro-Harmonix Golden Throat series: The Deluxe model sports a built-in 25-watt power amp.

Electro-Harmonix Bassballs.

Kustom made only about 100 Bags, and the talk box went on to more widespread popularity as the floor-mounted unit made by sound reinforcement pioneer Bob Heil. Heil met Walsh in '73 after Joe had his big hit "Rocky Mountain Way," which featured an extended talk box solo played on a unit built by his equipment manager, a guy known as "Kringle." Heil and Walsh brainstormed the idea of producing a commercial talk box, and a year later the Heil Talk Box hit the market. Bob later designed the talk box heard round the world: The rig Peter Frampton used on his stupefyingly popular '76 LP, Frampton Comes Alive.

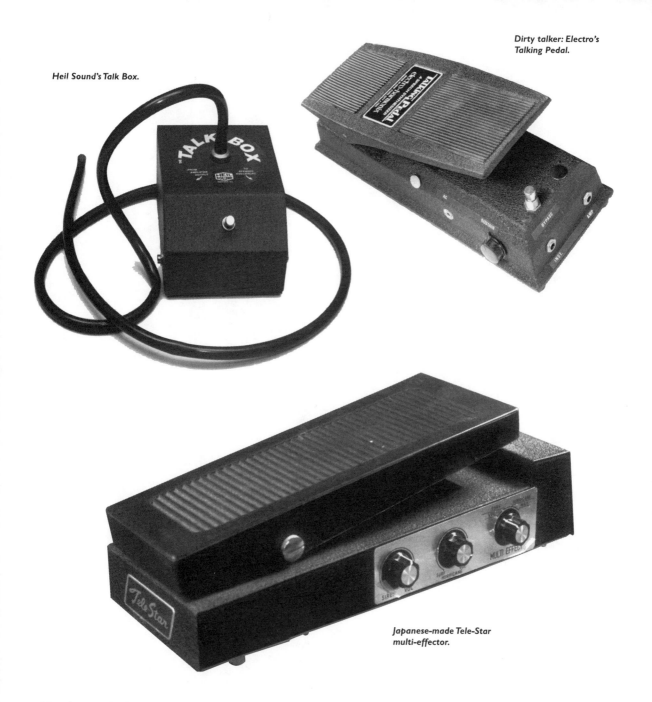

Heil Sound's Talk Box.

Dirty talker: Electro's Talking Pedal.

Japanese-made Tele-Star multi-effector.

Other talk boxes of the period included Dean Markley's Da Box, Voice Box, and Mighty Mouth, and Electro-Harmonix's Golden Throat series. The original Golden Throat featured an Electro-Voice driver, while the Golden Throat II used a cheaper version. Both sported an internal light bulb that acted like a variable resistor to prevent frying the driver. E-H's Deluxe Golden Throat packed its own 25-watt power amp.

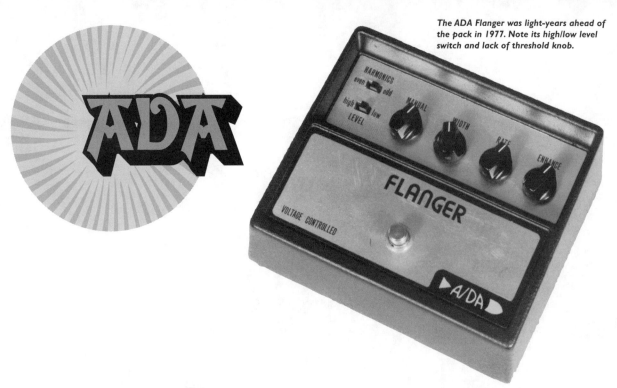

Analog Digital Associates was founded in 1975 by David Tarnowsky, a keyboardist and philosophy major turned electronics engineer who first dipped into musical electronics while working with Seamoon. Though ADA was initially involved in medical electronics, Tarnowsky's grasp of the emerging bucket-brigade technology quickly made ADA a major force in musical effects. Following their successful Flanger and Final Phase pedals (Pat Travers was an early Flanger endorser), ADA got into rackmount analog effects in the early '80s with the STD-1 Stereo Tapped Delay and TFX-4 (flanger, chorus, doubler, and echo) before moving into digital effects when the technology allowed. ADA was also first with a programmable tube guitar preamp, the MP-1.

Dave Tarnowsky's Story

I grew up in Southern California, played keyboards in an R&B band that made a small local splash when I was in junior high, and majored in philosophy at UC-Berkeley. After graduation I was a car mechanic for a while before becoming the house keyboard player at a recording studio in Emeryville [near Berkeley]. I moved on to medical electronics in 1976 and musical electronics a year later. I designed a flanger for a company called Seamoon, which had already established itself with the Funk Machine. When Seamoon folded, I decided to produce an improved flanger.

I'd heard about a new chip made by Reticon called the SAD1024 that did things better than a phase shifter, so I requested some samples and figured out how to use it. A lot of things had to be designed in those days, because nothing was known about what musical effects would work. One of the things I discovered was that we needed a wide-range voltage-controlled clock oscillator, and it also had to follow a particular semi-logarithmic pattern in order to sound like a rotating speaker. It took about a month to design, and that's the circuit we used in the ADA Flanger.

While I was working on the flanger, MXR came out with their Auto Flanger, which used an AMD 182-stage bucket-brigade device. It barely flanged at all. Tychobrahe also predated us with their Pedal Flanger. Those were the only other solid-state flangers that I knew about at the time. The Electro-Harmonix Electric Mistress came out sometime after ours was introduced.

We actually put our prototype Flanger into a wah-wah-type pedal and showed it at NAMM [the National Association of Music Merchants trade show], but we never produced that model. We immediately went with the square, cast-aluminum box. The first production Flangers showed up in June 1977, and we built them until 1981. The initial model went through a few board revisions. May 9, 1978, was the last date for the Reticon SAD1024 chip before we switched over to the Matsushita/Panasonic MN3010. We also changed to an internal transformer in October 1979. We built Flangers for nine months with internal transformers and then for two months with a circuit board designed for an internal transformer, but shipped with an AC

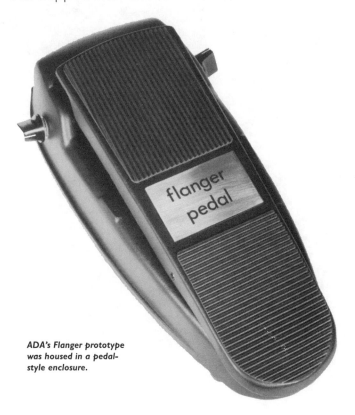

ADA's Flanger prototype was housed in a pedal-style enclosure.

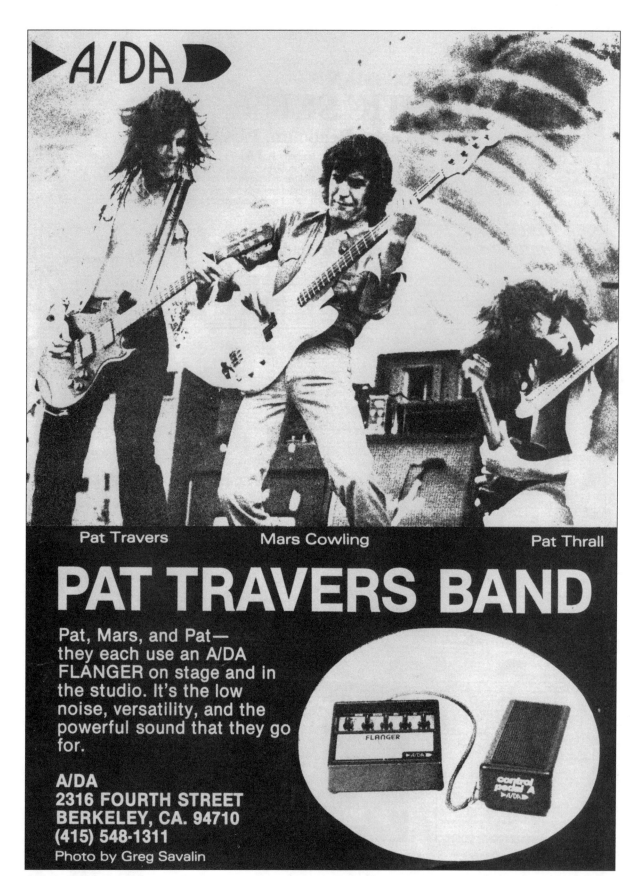
38

adapter because we couldn't get the transformers soon enough. When we exhausted that board run, we were ready to use the MN3010 chip. The SAD1024 had less headroom than the 3010, so I had designed a simple diode-limiting compressor to use with it. We later realized that the compressor enhanced the sound, so we kept it in the circuit when we changed to the 3010. The only drawback with the 3010 was that it wouldn't sweep over a wide range, so we had to experiment with differential coupling and the shape of the clock pulses in order to make the 3010 sweep over the 35-to-1 range that we'd achieved with the 1024.

The Final Phase evolved from the same-name pedal by JXL.

That wide sweep range is one of several features that set the ADA Flanger apart. Most companies were using a 10- or 15-to-1 sweep range, but our flanger would reach way down into the gutter and then sweep up and sound like it was disappearing over the horizon. Another difference was the compressor, which squeezed the sound a bit, and lastly was the way we did positive feedback with the enhance control and the odd/even harmonics switch.

We also used a pre-emphasized, highly tailored bandpass filter in the feedback circuit. We added a distortion component when the bandpass signal goes back into the compressor, which causes it to clip only the regenerated signal. That's what gives the Flanger that nice, crusty sound. The harmonics just jump right out. Unlike other devices, the Flanger's delay line isn't clipping or compressing. It's actually the feedback loop being conditioned and feeding a limiter that squares it up a bit and gives it some grind when you jump on it. That's how we got our distinctive tone.

The idea for the Final Phase came from the same person who had turned me on to the bucket-brigade devices. He had mathematically generated a transfer equation for a higher-Q bandpass or phase-shift filter. Most phase shifters

39

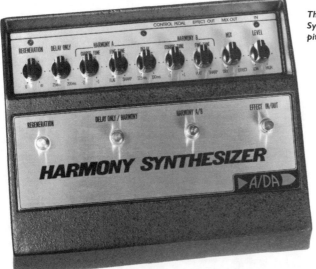

The super-rare Harmony Synthesizer was an analog pitch transposer.

have a Q of about 1/2, but this one had a Q of 1, which meant its notches were considerably steeper. ["Q" refers to the width of a filter circuit's resonant peak. A high-Q filter's is narrow and high-amplitude; a low-Q's is wide with a lower amplitude.]

When it swept, it actually detuned in pitch like a flanger does if you just listen to the delayed signal. I played around with his formula and eventually came up with a Weinbridge filter that would execute the math. I had a problem figuring out how to sweep it, though, so he came up with a modified bootstrap phase shifter that was sweepable using opto-isolators. It wasn't a stable circuit, however, so I went over to a pulse-modulated design. That's the one we manufactured in quantity.

The Final Phase, which we introduced on January 6, 1978, was a ten-stage phase shifter with a Q of 1. When you regenerated that circuit using positive feedback, it

became very flange-like. It was actually a distortion box and a phase shifter, because once you created the harmonics from the diode distortion generator, you had a lot to play with in terms of notching. It added a real gutteral growl to the phase shift. It also had a random sweep modulator that would modulate the sine wave, speeding it up and slowing it down and adding sine waves on top so it sounded like a random pattern.

Our only other stompbox was the Harmony Synthesizer. It was actually the world's only analog pitch transposer, but we called it a "synthesizer" because it synthesized harmony. That turned out to be a marketing problem for us because synthesizers had just started showing up and people thought it was a keyboard. It looked similar to the Flanger and Final Phase, but it was larger—11 inches deep and a foot across. Robert Fripp owns two of them, but they're actually quite rare because we shipped only about 800.

After that we became involved with rack gear. We designed the STD-1, a

THE "STUDIO QUIET" FLANGER

The **A/DA FLANGER** is a low noise electronic flanger capable of producing a broad range of sound colorations, dramatically enhancing the effect of any amplified musical instrument, voice or percussive instrument. Astounding effects such as rotating speakers, chilling vibrato, "jet" sounds, resonance modification, intensified studio flanging and incredible filter matrices, to name a few, suggest that experimentation will certainly find the sound you have been looking for.

The term "flanging" refers to the technique of manually varying the speed of two tape recorders independently with the same program material, while mixing down in recording studios. The **A/DA FLANGER** electronically simulates varying speed in real time, during the performance.

Some of the unique features that make the **A/DA FLANGER** the most advanced flanger available today include:

- Special circuitry that eliminates the characteristic buzzing noise of all other electronic flangers. The **A/DA FLANGER** is studio quiet!
- Even/Odd Harmonic emphasis switch which offers either a ringing hollow tube sound or a coarse jet-like sound. In the Odd position an electric bass develops 3-dimensional resonance boosts.
- A true voltage controlled sweep input that can take a 0 to 15 volt control voltage or the **A/DA CONTROL PEDAL A.**
- An automatic sweep that varies between 0.1 to 25 seconds for a complete sweep cycle.
- A rugged cast aluminum case and recessed controls that can withstand even the most demanding concert tour.
- AC/DC converter included.

Suggested retail price is $199.95 for the **A/DA FLANGER** and $39.95 for the **A/DA CONTROL PEDAL A.** 1 year full warranty.

Note the Flanger's odd threshold knob in this early promo.

ANALOG/DIGITAL ASSOCIATES, 2316 FOURTH STREET, BERKELEY, CA 94710
[415] 548-1311

multi-tap delay line that was used to double and create ambient effects including spatial location, and the TFX-4, which offered flanger, chorus, doubler and echo effects— one at a time. Next came a rackmount digital delay, which we offered in three delay times—640 milliseconds, 1.28 seconds, and 2.56 seconds. Later we introduced a low-end rackmount digital delay called the S-1000, and then we came out with a dual-effects unit that provided simultaneous flanger or chorus *with* echo or doubler. Following that we came out with a pitch transposer and a programmable graphic EQ. Then we started the programmable tube preamp market with our MP-1. We were the conceivers of that niche.

ARBITER

In late 1966 a circular stompbox called the Fuzz Face hit Britain's music scene. Designed and built by London's Arbiter Music, the Fuzz Face used two NKT-275 germanium transistors and featured volume and fuzz controls. Other versions were fitted with either BC 108 or SF 363E germanium transistors or BC 183 C silicon transistors.

The Fuzz Face has long been associated with Jimi Hendrix. The first photos of him playing through one were snapped in London's Marquee Club on January 24, 1967, and Hendrix continued to use Fuzz Faces—mostly in live performance—for the remainder of his career.

Arbiter's product line also included the Fuzz Wah and Fuzz Wah Face pedals (featuring CryBaby-style enclosures), Soundimension magnetic-drum echo units (including a model called the Soundette made for Fender), and Sound City amplifiers.

Ivor Arbiter oversaw his company's evolution from music store to major manufacturer of amplifiers and effects, and finally to its current status as Britain's largest musical-instrument distributor. Jim Dunlop currently produces the Dallas-Arbiter Fuzz Face.

Ivor Arbiter's Story

I started in the music business repairing saxophones in 1946 when I was 16. In '56 or '57 I opened my first shop, called Paramount Music, in the middle of London. It was a typical music store of the period until we began getting a demand for guitars. Bill Haley and Tommy Steele were big at that time, and there was this huge demand for anything that looked like a guitar. People didn't play them, they would *wear* them.

Arbiter-built Soundimension Echo.

Arbiter Fuzz Face flanked by Dallas-Arbiter Fuzz Wah Face (L) and Sound City Wah Face pedals.

You couldn't get guitars in England in 1958, so I borrowed a van from my best mate, who was in the gambling business, and went over to Holland and started buying guitars. From there on, the whole guitar thing started, and that's how we got into distribution. We started supplying other stores with guitars, and I was spending four nights a week on the ferry coming back from Holland with a couple of hundred guitars each trip. That led to another retail shop that we opened in London called Drum City, which was the first drum-only shop of its type in the U.K.

We opened a store called Sound City around the beginning of 1960. It was a very formative place—all the local guitarists used to go there. That's where we developed Sound City amplifiers. We also started importing Ludwig drums. I got Ringo for Ludwig—that was my claim to fame at the time.

We also set up Arbiter Electronics during that time and began producing various amplifiers and effects

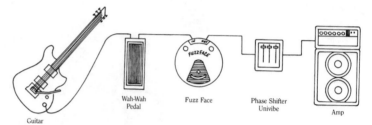
You could hardly go wrong with this classic setup.

units. It was the Hiwatt period—Marshall was just starting. Hiwatt's founder, Dave
Reeves, made the U.K. amp
industry happen for all of us
at the time. Jim Marshall
should go and put flowers on
his grave.

Arbiter Electronics started
making echo units and
octave dividers and things
like that. One day I said,
"Can't we make a fuzz unit
with a different shape?" I saw
a microphone stand with a
cast-iron base, and I said,
"Why don't we make it

round so it won't slip? Hence
the Fuzz Face, which had
some very nice sounds.
Hendrix especially liked it.
Jimi used to visit the Sound
City shop a lot, and he got
his first Fuzz Face there or
from Manny's in New York.

In 1968 we became a
publicly owned company
called Arbiter and Western.
We wound up with bingo
halls and a place called
Caesar's Palace at Lewton,
which I ran for three years. It
was a workingman's club
with cabaret, and that's

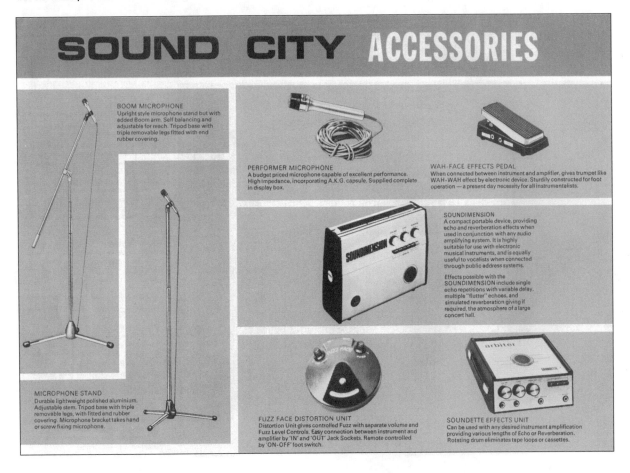

SOUND CITY ACCESSORIES

BOOM MICROPHONE
Upright style microphone stand but with added Boom arm. Self balancing and adjustable for reach. Tripod base with triple removable legs fitted with end rubber covering.

MICROPHONE STAND
Durable lightweight polished aluminium. Adjustable stem. Tripod base with triple removable legs, with fitted end rubber covering. Microphone bracket takes hand or screw fixing microphone.

PERFORMER MICROPHONE
A budget priced microphone capable of excellent performance. High impedance, incorporating A.K.G. capsule. Supplied complete in display box.

WAH-FACE EFFECTS PEDAL
When connected between instrument and amplifier, gives trumpet like WAH-WAH effect by electronic device. Sturdily constructed for foot operation — a present day necessity for all instrumentalists.

SOUNDIMENSION
A compact portable device, providing echo and reverberation effects when used in conjunction with any audio amplifying system. It is highly suitable for use with electronic musical instruments, and is equally useful to vocalists when connected through public address systems.

Effects possible with the SOUNDIMENSION include single echo repetitions with variable delay, multiple "flutter" echoes, and simulated reverberation giving if required, the atmosphere of a large concert hall.

FUZZ FACE DISTORTION UNIT
Distortion Unit gives controlled Fuzz with separate volume and Fuzz Level Controls. Easy connection between instrument and amplifier by 'IN' and 'OUT' Jack Sockets. Remote controlled by 'ON-OFF' foot switch.

SOUNDETTE EFFECTS UNIT
Can be used with any desired instrument amplification providing various lengths of Echo or Reverberation. Rotating drum eliminates tape loops or cassettes.

where I did a lot of my sound developments. It was very useful because we had a six- or eight-piece band, and I was there about six nights a week. We used to try out everything. The company eventually ran into some difficulties, and we sold the gambling side of the business to Ladbrokes and I went over to Dallas Musical Instruments. That's how Dallas-Arbiter got started. I stayed there for five years; we produced Sound City amplifiers, Hayman drums, and the Fuzz Face and other effects.

I left Dallas in 1975 to set up CBS-Arbiter. Dallas bought Vox because they'd lost Fender, and then Dallas went broke and CBS and I bought what was left of Dallas, so we got Vox back again. Then I sold Vox to Rose-Morris. Fender is now our largest side, and we also distribute DigiTech, Sabian, Vic Firth, and Remo, as well as our own line of band instruments.

DAN ARMSTRONG

Guitarist, luthier, effects pioneer—all describe Dan Armstrong, a designer whose credits include Ampeg's clear-plastic guitars, Armstrong amps, and a series of plug-into-your-ax effects boxes called the Red Ranger, Orange Squeezer, Yellow Humper, Green Ringer, Blue Clipper, and Purple Peaker. The Orange Squeezer was the compressor of choice for Steely Dan and Doobie Brothers guitarist Jeff "Skunk" Baxter: "One of my favorite boxes is the old Dan Armstrong Orange Squeezer," he told *Guitar Player* in 1992.

"It's probably the greatest guitar compressor I've ever heard."

Dan still invents and performs. His most recent ventures have included designing a series of speaker cabinets for Cerwin-Vega and honing his guitar chops in an organ trio that gigs around Southern California. WD Music Products currently makes the Blue Clipper, Green Ringer, Orange Squeezer, Purple Peaker, Red Ranger, and Yellow Humper.

Dan Armstrong's Story

The first effect I ever heard was tremolo, and the first tremolo unit I owned was a DeArmond. It was a late-'40s device that used an electric motor driving an eccentric wheel to shake a little vial of mercury back and forth, opening and closing the circuit. Was that ever analog! Then Fender came out with their electronic tremolo, which was much smoother and neater. The next effect I heard was reverb. I remember a guy named Bill Fisher who owned something called a Hammond Reverb Speaker. It had an internal reverb that used what looked like a door spring hung in a big arc inside the cabinet. It was designed to be used with a Hammond organ, but this guy had adapted it to use with his guitar.

The Green Ringer was Armstrong's first effect, though the Musitronics logo denotes a later version.

The first guitar amp with reverb that I remember was a Maestro accordion amp made by Gibson. This was in '62, and reverb really began about there. The next device was the Maestro Fuzz-Tone, which I heard in a music store when I was on the road. It was an interesting device. A 45-rpm record that came with the Fuzz-Tone demonstrated it sounding like a trombone and a saxophone and all these other things, but it wasn't pitched as a rock and roll device.

I had a guitar-repair store on 48th Street in New York in '65 when the Rolling Stones did "Satisfaction." That made the Fuzz-Tone a really desirable gadget, and before you knew it, there were all kinds of copies of the Maestro from Japan and Italy.

I started making my little boxes in London in 1973. That's where I met George Merriman, who was the electrician for the Rainbow Theater. He was an American, and we were both from Pittsburgh.

When I was working with Ampeg on the plastic guitars I got a device called the Scrambler from some outside engineers. It was an interesting gadget, sort of like a ring modulator. The idea was good but the design wasn't, so it just didn't sell very well. The only effect people knew about was fuzz, so they tried to use the Scrambler like a fuzz. It would sort of do that, but it would do a lot of other things too.

I told George Merriman about the Scrambler, and he said, "Oh, I know what that is. I'll make you one." So he made this gadget that was like a Scrambler, except that it worked right. We tinkered with it a little bit and named it the Green Ringer. It would play an octave up or one or two octaves down, and do all kinds of tricks. We put it in a little box that plugged into a guitar, and then we decided to see what else we could make in the same size box. I decided on a distortion device, and George came up with the Blue Clipper. About the time we

Purple Peaker EQ.

Blue Clipper distortion.

were just starting to market it, a guy from MXR came to England to show off their new phase shifter. He saw our box and went, "Man, how did you do that?" MXR then copied our Blue Clipper line for line and called it the Distortion Plus. The only change they made was adding a tone control, but they left out one offset resistor that gave the Blue Clipper more presence in the mix.

Next we wanted to make a booster similar to the Electro-Harmonix LPB-1. I asked George if he could make something like it that wasn't noisy, and he did. We called it the Red Ranger. It was an almost noiseless booster, and

we put a switch on it to change ranges from bass to treble, or all frequencies boosted.

I had spent some time with various graphic and parametric EQs that had just come on the market. I found that if you put a couple of peaks in the right place on a guitar, you could really improve the sound. We put that in a box, and it worked so well we did the same for bass. We called them the Purple Peaker and Yellow Humper respectively.

All along we had been working on the Orange Squeezer. That one was the most difficult. After screwing around with it for a couple of

Red Ranger booster.

Yellow Humper bass EQ.

years, we introduced it in 1974. We only used the little boxes because they were cheap and easy to get out on the market. We had intended to eventually put these effects in floor boxes, but they just never got there. Originally they were all made in England.

I met the Mu-Tron people in Frankfurt in '74. They were interested in making and selling our boxes in America, so we made a deal. When George went to America to help them with their production, we got to work on the Mu-Tron Octave Divider. We added a Green Ringer to it. It's still my favorite octave divider.

These were the only effects devices I really ever had on the market. George Merriman was really the electronics whiz, though. He was able to understand and execute guitar effects better than anyone I've ever met, but the music business wasn't good to him, or me either, as far as making enough money to make it worthwhile.

49

One of the most successful companies to sprout from the stompbox seed was DOD of Salt Lake City, Utah. Founder John Johnson and his partner David DeFranchesco entered the pedal biz in 1974 with little more than some ideas for improving sound and reliability. Beginning with a simple phase shifter, DOD was soon producing an array of effects boxes including the Mini-Chorus 460, Phasor 401, Envelope Filter 440, Phasor 490, Overdrive Preamp 250, FET Preamp 210, Phasor 201, Compressor 280, Phasor 401B, Chorus 690, Analog Delay 680, and Flanger 670.

These mechanical-footswitch boxes were replaced in 1981 by the Performer Series, which included the Wah Filter 545, Phasor 595, Compressor Limiter 525, Distortion 555, Delay 585, Flanger 575, and Stereo Chorus 565. This line was soon updated with the Sustain 515-A, Compressor Limiter 525-A, Wah Filter 545-A, Distortion 555-A, Stereo Chorus 565-A, Flanger 575-A, Delay 585-A, Phasor 595-A (a 6-stage design capable of 1,080 degrees of phase shift), and the Octoplus 535-A, which could produce a tone an octave below, a 12th below, and two octaves below the original note.

In 1982 DOD came out with the FX series: the Harmonic Enhancer FX85, American Metal FX56, Bi-FET Preamp FX10, Phasor FX20, Super Distortion FX55 (later called Supra Distortion FX55B), Envelope Filter FX25, Delay FX90, Stereo Chorus FX60 (later called the FX65), Overdrive Plus FX500 (renamed the FX50B), Stereo Flanger FX75, Stereo Reverb FX45, Swell Pedal FX15, Compressor Sustainer FX80B, Gate/Loop FX30B, and Stereo Phasor FX20B.

DOD/DigiTech's early '80s digital pedals included the PDS 1000 and PDS 2000 digital delays, PDS20/20 Multi Play, PDS 3000 Pedal Verb, and the PDS 1002 Two Second Digital Delay. Rackmount digital delays such as the RDS 900, RDS 1900 and RDS 3600 were introduced around this time. By 1986 the company had introduced multi-effects pedals such as the PDS 1700 Digital Stereo Chorus/Flanger and the PDS 1550 Programmable Distortion.

Despite becoming one of the world's foremost producers of digital effects, DOD—now a separate company from DigiTech—hasn't lost sight of its analog roots. Included among their 27 current stompbox flavors are the Juice Box overdrive, Meat Box (a subharmonic generator for bass), Ice Box stereo chorus, Vibro-Thang tremolo, and Gonkulator Ring Modulator.

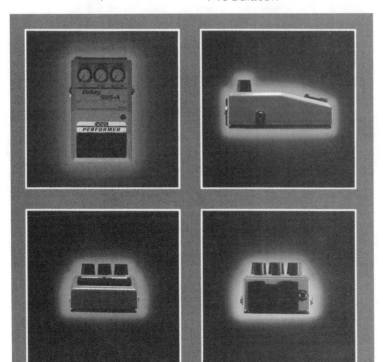

DOD's Performer series.

Envelope Filter
FX25

Noise Gate
FX30

Equalizer FX40

Sustain
515-A

PERFORMER

Delay
585-A

PERFORMER

Phasor
595-A

PERFORMER

Take Your Pick

The way it was in '79.

Whichever DOD product you choose you'll find consistent high quality design and materials.

Bi-FET Preamp
FX10

Phasor
FX20

Stereo Flanger
FX70

Distortion
FX55

John Johnson's Story

I started out as a professional musician playing in an R&B horn band like the Blues Brothers. We did nightclub tours all over the U.S. and Canada, but we couldn't make any money at it. At times we had to play heavier music—Led Zeppelin and Deep Purple stuff—and I found myself needing more effects. My old Dallas-Arbiter Fuzz Face just didn't have enough sustain when I used it with my Twin Reverb and Strat, though with a Les Paul and a Marshall it was fine.

I had my Fuzz Face modified by a few people, and one of them eventually became a business partner. Through that process we developed a distortion circuit that had a better sound. Once I quit touring, I decided to start a business based around the modifications that had been done to my equipment. People liked the sounds that I was getting, and it just made sense to start a business doing that. In 1975 we started building guitar effects.

Our first product was the 650 Phase Shifter. I didn't know how to make this stuff, but my partner did. I knew how it was supposed to sound and how to sell it. I had a marketing degree and music degree, and he had an engineering degree. The 650 Phasor and the 250 Overdrive were our two biggest sellers. Chorus was

53

Circa '82 FX series.

too because it was a new effect. As a guitarist, I'd played Leslies and knew a lot about them. Chorus sounded more like a Leslie to me than either phasing or flanging. I can't recall when I first heard chorus. It seems like we all just started building them at the same time.

I think you have to give Mike Matthews [of Electro-

Harmonix] credit for most of the effects deal. His company was really the first to produce a lot of boxes. The Small Stone in particular was a really good design, and it was very inexpensive.

I think the first phase shifter was made by Maestro. It was a big black box with orange, yellow, and blue switches for slow, fast, and

The seldom-seen Mini-Amp 650.

bypass. I didn't see MXR's phase shifter until '75, but we were already making our 601 Phasor.

Rack effects really sounded better than floor boxes, but people wanted to be able to access those sounds with their feet. Bob Bradshaw and others started making foot controllers to do that. Then we developed DSP multi-effects chips that could access a whole bunch of effects at once. We came out with the GSP-5, GSP-7, and GSP-21. It had 21 effects and could do 11 at one time. Then we built a foot controller for it. That was the start of moving things back toward pedals again. Korg came out with the A-5, which was about the same size as our controller but had the effects built right into it. Then we came out with the RP-1, and later the RP-5 and RP-10. Some players began plugging their old pedal effects into them. We gave

them a stand-alone floor box, and the next thing you know, they're plugging in Small Stones and whatever.

A lot of grunge guys and roots players wanted sounds that weren't so highly processed. Guitarists go through phases—from no effects to a lot of effects, and then back again. Everybody goes through that process; it's part of becoming a better player. I think some kind of processing is here to stay, whether it's amp simulators, delay, reverb, or chorus. There's always going to be a need for that stuff because people like to sweeten their sound.

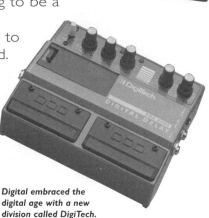

Digital embraced the digital age with a new division called DigiTech.

55

ELECTRO-HARMONIX

Founded in 1968 by electrical engineer and musician Mike Matthews, Electro-Harmonix exploded onto the effects scene with a stunning variety of great-sounding, innovative stompboxes. Beginning with a simple, one-transistor preamp/booster called the LPB-1, Electro-Harmonix was soon offering dozens of sheet-metal boxes with nutty names like Bad Finger, Mole, Soul Kiss, Screaming Tree, and Bad Stone.

One of Electro's best-loved products was the Small Stone phase shifter. Designed by David Cockeral, one of several E-H engineers, the Small Stone sounded astonishingly cool and was cheaper than its competition. As a MXR co-founder Keith Barr once said, "Whoever came up with that thing deserves a silver star."

The Cockeral-designed Electric Mistress flanger was another late-'70s mainstay. It was followed by the Deluxe Electric Mistress, designed by E-H engineer Howard Davis. Robin Trower reported having two Mistresses on his pedalboard—one for a double-tracking effect, the other for flange.

The Big Muff π was E-H's most famous distortion device. Developed at a time when guitarists wanted (or at least *thought* they wanted) clean sustain, the Big Muff was one of the first fuzzes to tout sustain over mere buzz. One of Electro's wackiest

Early promo.

56

Eleven flavors of Electro-Harmonix and one mixer

effects was the Bob Bednarz-designed Frequency Analyzer, a hilariously anarchic pitch mutator that challenges anyone's effector skills.

Electro-Harmonix folded in 1981, but Russian-made versions of some of their most popular effects are back. As of 1996, Mike Matthews' New Sensor company has reintroduced the Small Stone, Big Muff, Electric Mistress, and Memory Man.

Mike Matthews' Story

I attended Cornell University in New York, where I got a five-year degree in electrical engineering. I was also playing in a rock band, and I promoted a lot of rock and roll shows with early-'60s groups like the Isley Brothers, Byrds, Rascals, Lovin' Spoonful and the Mamas and Papas. Once I did a gig with the Isleys, and they asked me to quit school and go on the road with them. Jimi Hendrix also wanted to form a band with me. I stayed in school, though. That was my mistake.

After graduation I got my first gig, hustling computers for IBM. When you're a musician, though, you've got music in your blood. I was also married at the time, and my wife was kind of conservative. I started thinking about ways to make a lot of money quick so I could quit IBM and get back into playing.

I started out making a distortion unit for Guild called the Foxy Lady [designed by Bill Burcoe], right at the beginning of the distortion craze. Everyone at that time seemed to want a distortion-free sustainer, so I was also working on one with this great designer named Bob Meyer at Bell Labs [Meyer later joined Electro-Harmonix]. It turned out to be a very difficult thing, though, because you need a lot of gain when the signal is low, and then when you lose the signal, it's got to shut down without a bunch of pops and clicks.

57

Small Stones and Small Clone.

One of Bob's versions didn't have enough gain at the input, so he built a little one-transistor preamp to boost it. I flicked the switch on this preamp and went, "Wow." This was back in the days when guitar amps had lots of headroom. When you turned the knob up to 10, that's all you got. It would've been great if you could turn it up to 20 or 30, and that's what this booster did. I thought it would be a cool product, so I jumped on it. Getting into manufacturing isn't easy, but I was fortunate because this was really simple. It only had one transistor, one switch, a pot, and a few caps and resistors.

I called it the Linear Power Booster, or LPB-1, and I started selling them by mail order in 1968. The LPB-1 started to take off, so I quit IBM that same year. At the '68 NAMM show I had people waiting in line to buy them. One of them was Hartley Peavey. He later gave me credit by saying that one of his first hot amps had an overdrive section that was inspired by the LPB-1. We quickly had lots of offshoot products like the Screaming Bird, the Mole, and the Bass Booster. They were just different versions of the LPB-1.

After that our next big product was the Big Muff [introduced in '71], which Bob Meyer designed and I tuned. It still wasn't a distortion-free sustainer, but it had a lot of stages in which we rolled off the high harmonics and harshness. It also had a soft-clipping circuit that gave it a very smooth distortion. In certain settings it really had that Hendrix sound. Jimi bought a Big Muff from Manny's, and then I became friends with him when he was calling himself Jimmy James. He invited me to three different recording studios, and I saw him using the Big Muff on one of those sessions. Carlos Santana bought one from me by mail

order. I still have his check with the bongo drums on it. When we came out with the battery-powered Freedom amp, Ike Turner bought one and a Big Muff. The Freedom amp became real hot for us but, unfortunately, we used speakers made by CTS. When their workers went on strike, we had all this inventory piling up that we couldn't complete. We finally got one last run of speakers and then stopped making the amp. It was just too much of a pain in the neck.

The three pedals featured here are the (L-R) Queen Triggered Wah, Hotfoot, and the wacky Talking Pedal.

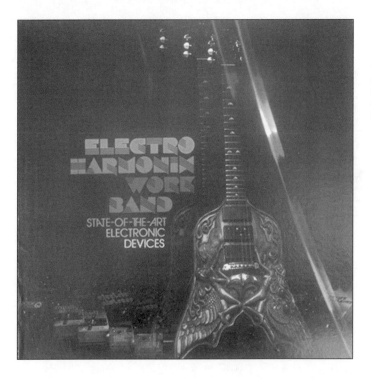

Which '70s album featured the greatest number of EH effects? Easy, the Electro-Harmonix Work Band's State-of-the-Art Electronic Devices.

Next we got involved in developing a phase shifter. The first company with a phaser was Oberheim, who made it for Maestro. Then MXR came out with the Phase 90, and that became a really hot product. The Bad Stone was our first phase shifter. One of the circuits we cooked up for it had some accidental feedback, which perked up the harmonics and gave it a real swishy and exaggerated sound. Then we came up with a new circuit that used transconductance op amps and didn't need any trimpots. By incorporating the Bad Stone's feedback feature we came up with the Small Stone.

60

Three versions of Memory Man.

A lot of companies concentrated on getting rid of every bit of circuit noise, but there were attack and interesting effects in the noise region. One of our secrets was leaving the noise in so musicians could get the most out of the effect.

Because it didn't have as many parts, we were able to offer the Small Stone at half the price of the Phase 90. Our whole philosophy was to build products at prices musicians could afford. Of course, packaging was not our forte—our stuff was always in those sheet-metal boxes. But we ended up taking over the phase-shifter market. At our peak we were making 6,000 to 8,000 units a month. If we could have made more, we could have sold them.

We were also the first on the market with a low-cost analog delay, called the Memory Man. The first ones, designed by Bob Meyer, used noisy Reticon chips, but when Panasonic came out with a bucket-brigade device, we jumped right on it. Howard Davis designed our second series of echoes—the Stereo Memory Man and the Stereo Memory Man with chorus—around the Panasonic chips. They were quiet, and they had that syrupy sound. Around that time we brought out the Electric Mistress and then the Deluxe Electric Mistress. Cockeral designed the original Mistress, while Davis did the later versions.

The stick-in-your-mouth Soul Kiss was a tasty wah.

Electro's hard-to-find Poly Flange with Clone Theory chorus and Super Replay sampler.

We had millions of dollars worth of orders, but right at that time karaoke machines were getting popular, and Roland and Ibanez were getting into the effects business. Suddenly Panasonic stopped shipping chips to us. We were only able to get a few here and a few there, and we lost our chance to sell tens of thousands of Memory Mans.

When digital technology came out we introduced the Two-Second Digital Delay, which was another David Cockeral design. It was the first digital echo for the mass market. That gave me the idea that if you had a little more memory, you could lay down some tracks and jam with yourself. That led to the 16-Second Digital Delay, which we introduced in '82.

Frequency Analyzer freakout.

Around the time we were cut off by Panasonic, we had just bought a new building. We were being squeezed by not being able to fill our echo orders, and this gang of union racketeers started trying to organize our employees. They had tried it a couple of years earlier, but the workers weren't interested. They said, "Look, Mike, join us and we'll show you how to work this. You just give us a little money and we'll help you." I refused, and they came down again in '81 when I was financially weaker. Again, our people rejected them. We had about 200 workers, and only six wanted to join. When the union saw they couldn't organize the company, they sent down a gang of hired ex-cons. One morning there were about 30 of them on the street, armed with clubs. They beat up everybody who tried to come in to work. The cops wouldn't do anything because it was a "labor problem." I called a newscaster at NBC and told him the story. He called me back the next day and told me they filmed it with hidden cameras. They showed it on the news for three days straight, and it was a major story in New York. The union pulled away after that, but it weakened me further and the bank called in their loan. That was the end of Electro-Harmonix.

The Hotfoot's flexible shaft allowed you to turn any control with your foot.

FENDER

Leo Fender was amazing. He got guitars right, he got amps right, and he perfected what was probably Fender's greatest contribution to guitar effects—reverb. Leo didn't invent spring reverb, but his circa-'62 Reverb Unit set the standard for guitar-oriented reverb.

Surf music pioneer Dick Dale tells this story about its origin:

"The reverb came about after I explained to Leo Fender and Freddy Tavares that I didn't have natural vibrato in my voice and my live show was 95 percent singing. I wanted to sustain my voice like you can a piano note by pushing down on the sustain pedal. The note just hangs there. I told Leo that I had a Hammond organ at home, and it had a button that gave you a reverb sound that was closer to what I wanted. Leo built a device that

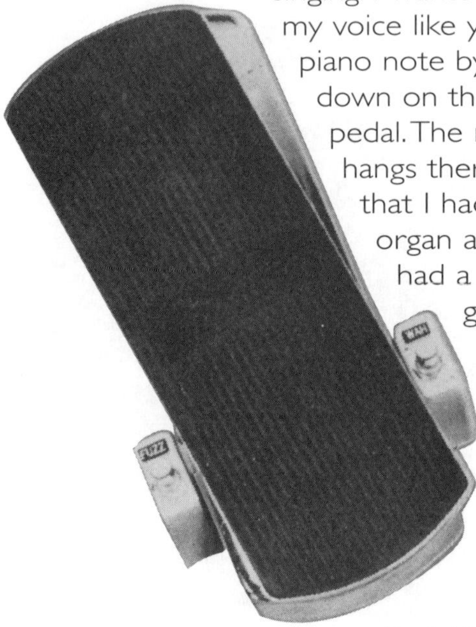

New for '68 was Fender's Fuzz-Wah

had a Hammond Organ Company spring tank mounted inside. When I plugged a Shure Dynamic birdcage microphone into it, I was able to sing and sound like Elvis. That was the birth of the Fender reverb. Later, when I plugged my Stratocaster into the reverb and played some of my shows, it was the icing on the cake."

Other short-lived Fender-made reverbs included the Solid State Reverberation Unit, Echo-Reverb, and the Variable Echo Reverb. Instead of tape, the latter two used a rotating metal-coated disk that was electrostatically charged in record mode and spun past stationary playback heads. Fender even offered a large hand-held microphone with built-in reverb, the model F-570.

Reverb wasn't the first effect Fender offered. A few years earlier, in 1958, Fender began distributing the EccoFonic tape echo. That was the same tube-powered unit that EchoSonic amp inventor Ray Butts said had infringed on his trademark. In

STUDIO DELUXE SET ·······

CHAMP STUDENT SET ······

ECCOFONIC ················

Eddie Bush   The Kings IV

The choice of Leading Artists everywhere

'63 Fender introduced their own tape echo, the Solid-State Electronic Echo Chamber, and in '66 they came out with the Echo-Reverb, which had three fixed delay settings and used an electrostatically charged rotating metal disk instead of a tape loop. Another twist on tapeless delay was Fender's 1967 Soundette, which used magnetic-drum technology.

Though Fender had a phase shifter in 1967—called simply the Phaser—their best-known Doppler device was the Vibratone, produced from 1967 to '72. Designed for keyboards, the two-speed Vibratone was based on the Leslie concept (CBS owned Leslie at the time), but it had a lightweight foam baffle that rotated around a single 10" guitar speaker. Its Tolex-covered enclosure was also better suited for rock and roll environments than the

1961 Fender Reverb catalog blurb.

New!

FENDER REVERB UNIT—Designed for use with all amplification systems, the new Fender Reverb unit offers the finest distortion-free reverberation.

Vibratone with Fender-Rhodes pianos at the Hollywood Bowl 1968.

Fender effects circa '76.

Phaser

Volume Foot Pedal

furniture-grade Leslie. Stevie Ray Vaughan used a Vibratone on "Cold Shot" and his Hendrix renditions.

Responding to the late-'60s fuzz frenzy, Fender introduced the Fuzz-Wah in 1968. The device originally sported a treadle that moved sideways for wah, but production Fuzz-Wahs were modified for up-and-down action. Outrigger switches selected fuzz, wah, or both. In 1974 Fender debuted a new,

Blender

sleeker Fuzz-Wah that featured fuzz blend and fuzz output controls. Last of Fender's fab fuzzes was the famous Blender, which featured controls for volume, sustain, tone, and blend, plus a second "tone boost" footswitch. Robin Trower reported using a Blender through an Electro-Harmonix Electric Mistress to get the rocket-ship sound on his 1977 album *In City Dreams*.

Fuzz-Wah

Tone and Volume

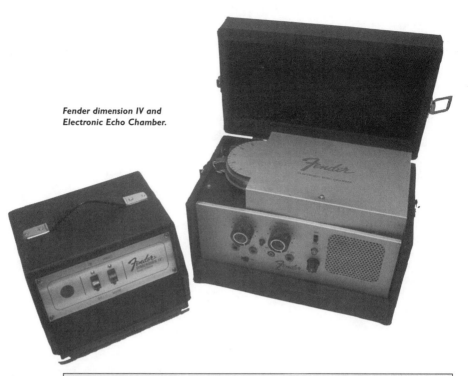

Fender dimension IV and Electronic Echo Chamber.

Normally conservative Fender got caught up in the spirit of the wacky '60s with the Orchestration+, a stand-mountable effects unit for horn players that offered trumpet, sax, bass, clarinet, tuba, contrabass, and "doo-wah" sounds. The main unit sold for $299.50, the pickup cost an additional $39.50, and the stand $16.50. Another sonic oddball was the Dimension IV, which featured reverb and the Tel-Ray-designed Ad-N-Echo delay system, which used an oil-filled can turned by an electric motor. And Fender's Special Effects Center was an all-in-one-box that offered fuzz, echo, reverb, and the mind-altering Dimension IV sound.

ACCESSORIES

FOOT SWITCHES
Heavy-duty single or double button foot switches. Single button designed for remote control of amplifier vibrato while double button controls both amplifier reverb and vibrato. Choose the one to fill your particular needs.

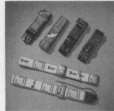

STRAPS & BELTS
Matching Fender-design straps and belts. Straps and belts are vinyl backed and available in a variety of colors. An eye-catching combo!

HUMBUCKING PICKUPS
High output double coil units fit most guitars and basses. Mounting hardware and instructions included.

UNIVERSAL STAND
Excellent stand for most amplifiers and P.A. heads. Convenient casters and heavily-plated metal components. Just right for the more compact, self-contained Fender amps such as Vibrosonic Reverb, Twin Reverb, and Pro Reverb.

HARDSHELL CASES
Strong and sturdy, plush lined cases. Covered with heavy vinyl fabric. Bound protective edges. Accessory compartments.

PATENT HEADS
Sets of individual machine tuning heads. Mounting hardware included. Chrome-plated tuning knobs.

AMP COVERS
To go places with your amp, pick a waterproof, tear and abrasion-resistant cover. Lined with soft flannel.

ECONOMY CASES
Softshell lined cases with reinforced sewn edges. Sturdy carrying handle and scuff-resistant material.

BRIDGE REPLACEMENT KIT
Six section bridge replacement kit for Telecaster guitars. The individual bridges are fully adjustable for length and height. Hardware and instructions included.

Fender effects circa '76.

Steve Ridinger's fuzz-flocked fuzzboxes were hot items on the Nixon-era guitar scene. Between 1971 and 1975, Ridinger & Associates produced a huge number of Foxx devices, many with "machine" in the name: Tone Machine, Power Machine, Loud Machine, OD Machine. The title was well-deserved; these were some of the gnarliest amp blasters ever made. Peter Frampton once said his favorite effect was an old Foxx fuzztone Elliot Randall gave him. "It's fantastic!" Frampton enthused. "It gives that sort of Hendrixy 'Stone Free' or 'Purple Haze' sound."

Steve Ridinger and ex-Foxx product manager Dick Norse provided their accounts of the Foxx years. Steve is currently the president of Danelectro, while Dick now owns a Southern California company that makes, among other things, valves for nuclear submarines and the Space Shuttles.

Dick Norse's Story

Steve Ridinger started out building effects in his garage as teenager. When I joined him in the summer of '73, he was 21, and he'd already been in business a couple of years. He played some guitar, but he was really more of an entrepreneur. He had gone to USC for a semester, but decided he could learn more doing it for himself.

I was working at Rockwell doing airframe design, and had just gotten my business degree and wanted to get into some kind of business. I handled everything at Foxx, including the purchasing and some of the

Flocked Foxxes: (L-R) Guitar Synthesizer I, O.D. Machine, and Clean Machine.

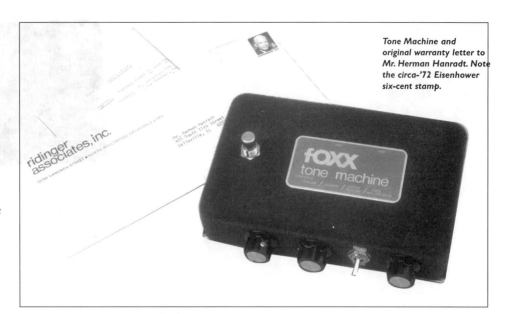

Tone Machine and original warranty letter to Mr. Herman Hanradt. Note the circa-'72 Eisenhower six-cent stamp.

engineering. We had some real good products-especially our Tone Machine, which was a fuzzer with octave sustain. When I joined, we were making the Tone Machine, Fuzz & Wah, Loud Machine, Down Machine [a wah pedal for bass], and the O.D. Machine, which was never a big seller for us, though the others were. Later we came out with the Foot Phaser and the Guitar Synthesizer [which had an envelope-follower function], and we also brought out a little practice amp called the Playola 10. Initially, Steve Ridinger designed all of our products, but the later stuff was designed by Doug Talley, whom I worked with for another 14 years after Foxx.

Ridinger was a nice little company. At our peak we were selling 12,000 units per quarter and had 2,000 dealers. In the first year I was there, our sales went from $263,000 to around $750,000, just by increasing capacity. That was big bucks for us. We started losing lots of dealers to the CryBaby pedal because we couldn't build our wah-wah fast

enough, but we were on good terms with Thomas Organ otherwise. Our wah units used the same little Japanese-made TDK inductor that Thomas used for the CryBaby, and I'd go in on quantity buys with them. That helped us keep our price down. To increase our production we started manufacturing in Mexico. We used one plant in Tijuana and another in Mexicali. All the guts were subassembled there, and we did the final assembly in the States.

Originally all the pedal casting was done in Mexico, but eventually I had the die-cast tooling done in El Monte, California. The flocking was done using epoxy and polyester filaments of varying lengths that were electrostatically drawn to the pedals. We would put six epoxy-coated bases in this chamber we'd made, and run 60,000 volts at very low amperage through the pedals. We had a blower that would suspend the filaments

69

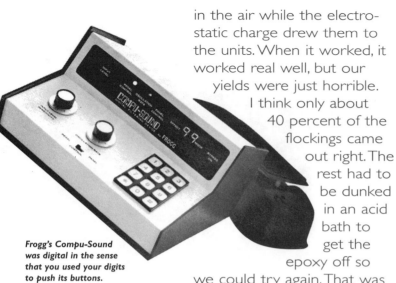

Frogg's Compu-Sound was digital in the sense that you used your digits to push its buttons.

in the air while the electro-static charge drew them to the units. When it worked, it worked real well, but our yields were just horrible. I think only about 40 percent of the flockings came out right. The rest had to be dunked in an acid bath to get the epoxy off so we could try again. That was something I never could get a handle on, and it didn't seem to be temperature- or humidity-related. Steve came up with the idea originally, and I kept trying to figure out ways to make it work better.

We sold Sears an unflocked black-painted version of our Fuzz & Wah, and we also sold some of our pedals under the Turtle brand. We private-labeled our stuff to other companies as well. There was a little cavity in the pedal that would take a nameplate, and I had lots of different plates for everybody. We sold the Foxx pedals to our dealers for $50 apiece, and they'd retail them for $99.95. Sears was selling the same thing for $49.95, and they were getting them from us for $27. That negotiation was pretty hairy.

50 stars-and-stripes Tone Machines were made in '72.

We were always trying to predict what every-body wanted. I don't know how well we succeeded. Foxx closed up in mid '75 and the company's assets were auctioned to someone in Chicago.

In the late '70s we started our own little effects skunk works called Frogg. We made a flanger, a phaser, a fuzz/wah, a micro fuzz, and a ring modulator. The micro fuzz's box was made by the Bud company and was the same size as MXR's. They wrote us a cease-and-desist letter about that. The micro fuzz was a great-sounding unit because we used Ridinger's design. Doug Talley added an octave-sustain feature, but we didn't sell very many.

We also had a thing called the Compu-Sound Guitar Computer. It was a digital filtering device, and by "digital" we meant you used your fingers to push the buttons. We took some license with that term, as well as with the statement that it used microprocessor technology. The Compu-Sound had 99 prepro-grammed sounds. You punched in a couple of num-bers and you got that sound. It worked great with a Wurlitzer keyboard, and it was used on the *Saturday Night Fever* soundtrack. We made and sold 100 of them, but it was a hard sell-$500 was a lot back then. At the '77 NAMM show, Frogg was one of four companies exhibiting a guitar synthesizer. We did that until we decided we didn't want to spend any more money trying to bring out the world's greatest guitar synth that nobody wanted.

Steve Ridinger's Story

I became interested in distortion boxes in high school during the early '60s, after hearing fuzz effects in songs by the Yardbirds and other bands. Vox had a little distortion device on the market, but I didn't have enough money to buy one so I just started tinkering around with circuits. Effects weren't so common in those days. There was the Maestro Fuzz-Tone, and later the Jordan Bosstone, but most players really didn't see them as necessities.

I built my first fuzz at age 13, and in '67 I decided to try

and make it a real business. I was 15 at the time, and my first product was called the Liverpool Fuzz Tone. My dad was an electronics engineer, and he helped me with it. I'd also read some articles about building your own fuzzbox in Popular Mechanics.

My distortion concept was that you took a single transistor gain stage and ran it into the input of the next stage. That didn't offer tremendous tonality, but you got lots of harmonics and distortion. You could look at the signal on a scope to see what part of the wave was distorting, and then tweak it until you got something you liked. It was pretty crude, but that's how I did it. I wouldn't call myself an engineer, but I knew that if I biased the transistor differently, we could get more gain.

The complete set in '74.

O.D. MACHINE
The unit that put 'overdrive' on the map. Dial-a-Boost, from 3 times to 30 times your power. Makes exciting controlled feedback effects possible. The longest sustain available with ANY device. We've clocked it as 5 minutes. You're welcome to challenge the record. PRICE: $69.95

LOUD MACHINE
Exquisite foot control of volume for all professionals, regardless of instrument. Built like a FOXX, too. PRICE: $42.95

FUZZ & WA & VOLUME (New)
Ah yes. Five inches high and the biggest in the business. Combines ALL the great tone machine features (longest variable sustain, active sustain, etc.) with the unique FOXX 4 position WA circuitry. You'll eat it up. PRICE: $99.95

WA & VOLUME MACHINE (New)
From mellow to brite to funky. Unique 4 position selector-switch gives you the sound of four different WA pedals in one. Unbelievable tone range and clarity. Designed by the man who designed the 'Vox Crybaby' six years ago. From Bangor to Pensacola and Ft. Worth to San Francisco this has rapidly become the fastest selling WA in the USA! PRICE: $64.95

WORLD FAMOUS TONE MACHINE
You've heard it again and again on recordings. Smoothest and longest sustain you'll ever hear. Plus FOXX exclusive active-sustain effect... adds a simulated octive to your instrument. You'll dig it. PRICE: $59.95

FOXX AMPLIFIED PRACTICE HEADPHONES

**Practice in private!
Tune up backstage!**
Solid state amplifier with full range 3" speakers. Frequency response **20** to **13,000** cycles... Complete mobility for warm-ups, practice anywhere, anytime without disturbing others... Adjust volume and tone with controls on your guitar... Also for electric keyboard... Allows you to practice without disturbing others... Two can listen at once... Simply plug in Monitor Phone. PRICE: $59.95

CLEAN MACHINE (New)
Use our selector dial for more, more and still more sustain. Gives you the cleanest sustain (or the dirtiest if that's what you want!) Plug one in! PRICE: $69.95

DOWN MACHINE
Two position selector switch allows bass or organ player to select 'mellow' or 'mellow plus' WA effects. The first and only WA-WA device for bass player and organist. By the designer of the 'Vox Crybaby.' PRICE: $69.95

Lay your SOUL on these!

MORE FOXX GOODIES ON THE BACK

SORRY, NO LONGER AVAILABLE......

FROGG

Frogg was a short-lived effects company started in the late '70s by ex-Foxx product manager Dick Norse.

The Liverpool used those big "top hat" germanium transistors, but later we switched to silicon for the Foxx stuff. We'd buy surplus transistors for three or four cents apiece—anything that had the right beta for the gain we needed.

I got orders for the Liverpool from several music stores in Hollywood, where I lived, but since I wasn't old enough to drive, I focused on stores that were within walking distance. Later I got eight or ten national distributors. Because I was in high school and didn't have the time to do assembly, I found an electronics company in Hollywood called WJS to build them. It was owned by a guy named Warren Jones, and he really helped us out because in those days we didn't have drill jigs or anything like that. I was doing everything with a hand drill.

We made about 2,000 to 3,000 Liverpools, and I tested each one in my bedroom. They retailed for $19.95, and didn't have any controls or even a footswitch—just a big bat-

handled toggle switch and a clip to attach it to your belt. It was a bright, heavy-sounding fuzz with lots of harmonics.

We also made a wah-wah back in '68 during the Liverpool days, but we didn't have a good housing for it. The one we used tended to tip back when you put your weight on it. I think I used the Foxx name then, but with one "x." We probably made only a couple hundred of those early wahs. When Foxx was established we started with the Tone Machine and added the Wa & Volume Machine about a month or two later. Originally the pedal housings came from DeArmond, but later we got someone to make a sand casting for it.

I was involved in the design of our first wah-wah, but we got help from some other people for the rest of our products. The Tone Machine was designed by a classmate of mine from Hollywood High School. His name was Rob, but I don't remember his last name. As far as I know that was the first fuzz unit with a switchable octave effect. I didn't even know how to spell octave then—that's why it's written "octive" on these boxes.

The Tone Machine was a really nice piece of work. Several boutique pedal companies have copied that circuit. Some have improved it. Tone Machines accounted for about 40 percent of the approximately 50,000 effects boxes that we made in our four-year history.

I started college at the University of Southern California at 17, but dropped out after the first semester to make musical products. Foxx was incorporated in 1970 after private investors put in about $20,000. We opened a storefront in North Hollywood and began producing our first effects in January '71.

My dad had some letterhead from an old consulting business called Ridinger & Associates, so I just used that name. During the day I went to music stores and took orders, and at night I supervised a crew of assembly people. This really burned me out, though, and eventually we went to just a day shift.

The idea for the nylon flocking came when I visited a gift show in 1970. I was looking for something to set apart our products, and this seemed like just the thing. We started with five colors—red, blue, black, yellow, and ugly lime green. Eventually we had eight different colors. In '72 we made about 50 Tone Machines in a stars-and-stripes design.

Foxx moved to larger facility in Chatsworth, California, in the summer of '72. In '73 we came up with the Fuzz & Wa & Volume Machine, which had a four-position selector to change the frequency response. It

was the first wah with that feature. We also had a power booster that was similar to an Electro-Harmonix LPB-1. Ours used a Maxwell House coffee-jar lid as an enclosure because we didn't want to pay for tooling. We bought the lids for about five cents each, but never made very many of those units.

Foxx was chronically short of cash, but that was probably more a result of my management inexperience than anything else. In '73 or '74 MXR entered the market and our sales suffered. Also, our new products in '74 and '75—which included oddball phasers and a "guitar synthesizer"—were rather esoteric and didn't sell well. For these reasons we closed the business in mid '75.

---

ridinger associates, inc.

May 1, 1972

IMPORTANT MODEL CHANGE AND PRICE CHANGE INFORMATION

Dear Dealer:

We have just introduced entirely new circuitry and product concept for three of our FOXX machines. They are the FOXX Wa Machine, FOXX Down Machine and FOXX Fuzz & Wa. These machines have been re-designed by the same man who designed the VOX "Crybaby" Pedal six years ago.

These machines contain the latest in engineering innovations and the new FOXX Wa Machine and the new FOXX Fuzz & Wa contain a revolutionary new four position selector switch that allows you to obtain distinctly new and different types of Wa sounds from funky to mellow to brite. It's like getting four pedals in one.

We invite you to try each of these three new machines. FOXX Down Machine contains a two position selector switch which gives exciting new effects for the bass, electric organ or other electronic instruments. The retail prices on these items are up slightly. The FOXX Fuzz & Wa now lists for $79.95--your cost $40.00. The FOXX Wa Machine now lists for $54.95--your cost $27.50 and the FOXX Down Machine now lists for $54.95--your cost $27.50.

Although prices have increased slightly to enable us to cover the increased material and labor costs involved in making these splendid machines, we are quite sure from initial sales reaction that these will prove to be the hottest selling items in your store. We suggest you get some of these machines in the store right away.

Most of our production run is sold on these models so we suggest you order soon. Please call us collect to place your new order for the new FOXX Wa Machine, Fuzz & Wa and Down Machine.

Best wishes,

Steve Ridinger
SR/rw

IBANEZ

The Ibanez story dates back to 1908, when Matsujiro Hoshino opened a book and stationery store in Nagoya, Japan. By 1932 Hoshino was producing guitars under the Ibanez name, and 30 years later the Hoshino Guitar Company purchased half interest in a small American guitar firm called Elger that had been importing guitars from Hoshino and other Japanese companies.

Ibanez hit pay dirt in '71 with their infamous line of Fender, Gibson, and Rickenbacker knockoffs, and by the mid '70s had added a line of effects pedals manufactured by Nisshin in Matsumota, Japan. Nisshin

This early Ibanez Fuzz & Wa screams "Foxx."

also made pickups for Matsumota's Fuji Gen Gakki, one of the companies that produced guitars for Ibanez. Nisshin used the name Maxon for their own effects, which were practically identical to the ones they made for Ibanez.

Marketing manager Roy Miahara describes Ibanez's early pedal efforts: "When Ibanez CEO Tom Tanaka saw the MXR stuff, we began making copies of it. In those days the yen was about 260 or 270 to the dollar. You didn't have to worry about marketing anything. You could just bring it over here and make tons of money on it. Nisshin made all of Ibanez's pedals, and they also owned the name Maxon. Ibanez was buying

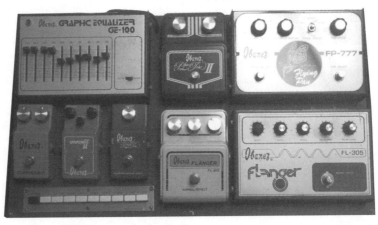

Late '70s in-store demo rig.

OVERDRIVES

COMPRESSOR & BLUBBER

FLANGERS

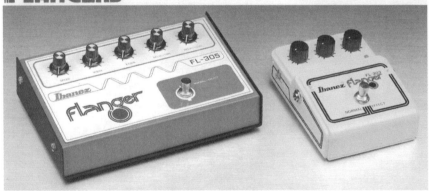

PHASE SHIFTERS

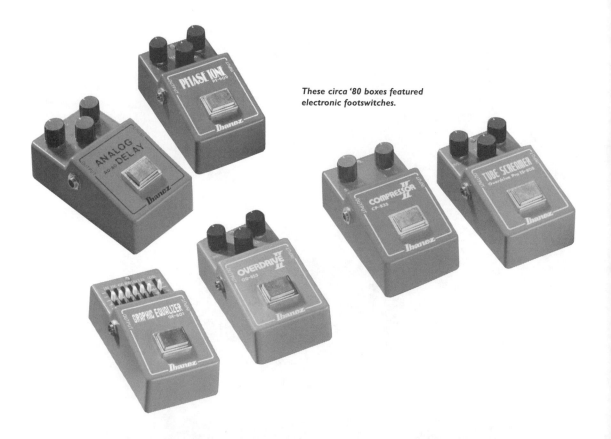

These circa '80 boxes featured electronic footswitches.

The 1982 line.

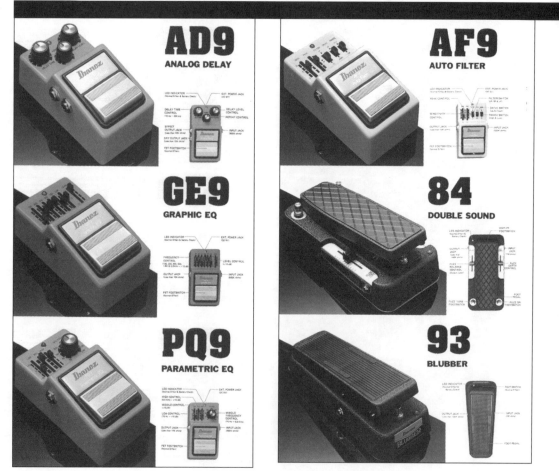

76

guitars from Fuji Gen Gakki, and Nisshin made the pick-ups and electronics. When they started getting into sound effects, we gave them ideas for what to build. I remember Nisshin's first wah-wah pedal worked backwards—it got bassier when you pushed the pedal down. We worked constantly to improve the pedals from our end. Nisshin had their own engineering staff, but they also used input from our engineers to design many of the pedals."

One of Ibanez's most famous effects was the TS-9 Tube Screamer, a medium-gain overdrive unit designed to emulate the sound of a tube amp. Designed by Nisshin in the early '80s and made legendary by Stevie Ray Vaughan and Eric Johnson, the TS-9 was essentially a repackaged version of an earlier Ibanez/Nisshin hit, the TS-808. The only electronic difference between them are the values of the two resistors in their output; a TS-808 has a 10kΩ resistor and a 100kΩ resistor, while the TS-9 uses 100kΩ and 470kΩ

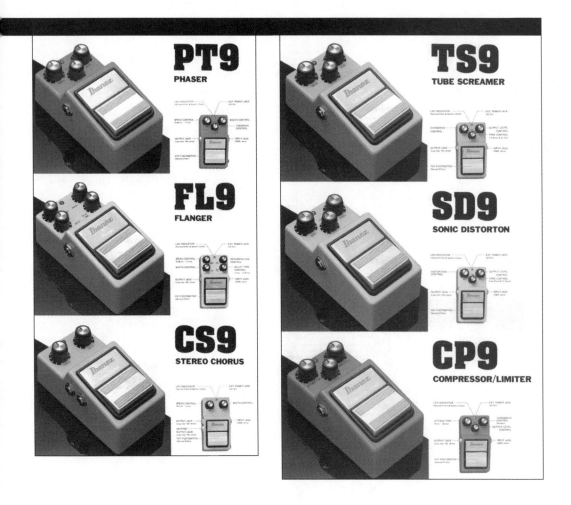

Three generations of Tube Screamers: TS-808 (center) flanked by a TS-9 (R) and a TS-10.

resistors. "I don't think I use the TS-9 the way they made it to be used," Stevie Ray told *Guitar Player* in 1983. "I have it set so it makes everything sound turned up."

Ibanez engineer John Lomas remembers that the TS-9's circuit was considered unstable, and that units were assembled with whatever parts were readily available. For example, some TS-9s were made with a special hi-fi dual op-amp called a TA 75558 instead of the more common 4558 listed in the circuit specs. Attempting to solve such "problems,"

Ibanez replaced the TS-9 with the TS-10, which featured an extra transistor plus a number of other circuit tweaks. Despite the upgrades, the TS-10 never attained the popularity of the TS-808 or TS-9, and some renegade tone-aholics would trade any of those boxes for Ibanez's less famous SD-9 Sonic Distortion. This pale-green powerhouse borrowed from the ProCo Rat and Electro-Harmonix Big Muff circuits, and it offered more distortion and bottom end than any of the TS-series pedals.

Maxon's version of the TS-808.

Maxon Roto Phase I is a repackaged Ibanez Phase Tone.

This TS-808 sports a smaller enclosure and a battery eliminator jack next to the input.

IBANEZ MULTI-EFFECTS SYSTEMS

As the relationship between the artist and electronics has matured the professional has seen a need for more sophisticated signal processing capabilities. He needs a system that is easily changed in live situations. It must be compact, easy to set up and yet flexible enough to accomodate his particular sound.

Ibanez was first to meet this challenge with the UE400 Rack System Series — professional quality rackmount processor systems. The response was tremendous. The UE400 Series have found their way into professional and semi-pro recording studios PA systems as well as musical instrument systems.

Ibanez continues to lead the way with the UE300 Floor System Series — a bold new format for multi-effect systems. And again, the response has been overwhelming. Clearly the time for Ibanez Multi-Effect Systems has come.

UE300 FLOOR SYSTEM SERIES

Each system in the UE300 series contains three integrated signal processors and an external loop for use with external processors. Each effect or the whole system may be switched in and out using the Q-1 silent switching system. The UE300 Series are AC powered and include multiple outputs for dimensional enhancement of the sound. LED's indicate the status of each effect and master control. Professional quality and roadability make the UE300 Floor System Series a unique solution for the pedal weary musician. Uniquely Ibanez.

UE400 RACK SYSTEM SERIES

The UE400 Rack System Series are the most advanced multi-effects systems in the industry. Four signal processors and an external loop capability are integrated into the most flexible package available. The Ibanez Insta-Patch switching system permits the artist to place each effect in any desired location — no patch cords are necessary. Changes in the Insta-Patch program are quick and easy, giving the artist a versatility never before realized.

Each UE400 System is AC powered and housed in a standard EIA 19 inch rackmount package. A remote footswitch provides foot control of all effects and system bypass. LED's on the rack unit and the remote footswitch indicate the status of each effect, the Insta-Patch system and master control. Multiple outputs are provided for enhanced dimensional effects.

The UE400 Rack System Series represents the leading edge of multi-effects system technology — maximum flexibility, easy utilization, and the professional quality that is Ibanez.

9

1983 introduction of the UE300
and UE400 series.

UE405 RACK SYSTEM

UE400 RACK SYSTEM

80

UE300 FLOOR SYSTEM

The UE300 Floor System utilizes a powerful trio of processors for guitars or bass. The exceptionally quiet Compressor/Limiter with variable attack time, the Tube Screamer for a myriad of tube amp sounds, and the Stereo Chorus, the latest time delay sound whose stereo outputs dimensionally enhance all of the effects of the UE300. The combination of Compressor/Limiter and Tube Screamer is ideal for creating smooth, ultra-sustained distortion. An external loop permits the artist to place additional processors between the Tube Screamer and Stereo Chorus. Q-1 silent switching is provided on all sections and on master control. The UE300 Floor System—today's most desired sounds in today's most advanced design.

SPECIFICATIONS

Comp/Limit. Compression Ratio	40 dB
Tube Screamer Max. Gain	+30 dB
Stereo Chorus	
Time Delay Range	3.2 – 8.5 ms
Input Impedance	
(Input, Effect Receive)	500K ohms
Output Impedance	
(Output 1, 2 and Eff Send)	<1K ohms
Dimensions	310(w) x 190(d) x 70(h) mm
Weight	1.9 kg, (4.2 lbs.)
Power Requirements	
	117 VAC, 60 Hz, 3.7 W
	220 – 240 VAC, 50 Hz, 5.2 W

UE303B FLOOR SYSTEM

The UE303B Floor System contains the three most popular processors for bass. The versatile Auto Filter for attack-driven automatic filtering, the Compressor/Limiter with variable attack time, and the Stereo Chorus/Flanger for an undulating bass sound. Stereo outputs enhance all of the effects of the UE303B when used with two amplifier systems. An external loop permits the artist to insert additional signal processors between the Compressor/Limiter and the Stereo Chorus/Flanger. The Q-1 switching system provides silent switching of all effects and master control. The UE303B—the most advanced processor system for bass, keyboards or guitar.

SPECIFICATIONS

Auto Filter Frequency Range	
	50 – 1 KHz (Low Range)
	100 – 2 KHz (High Range)
Comp/Lim Compression Range	40 dB
Stereo Chorus/Flanger Delay Range	
	1.0 – 12.8 ms (Flanger)
	3.2 – 8.5 ms (Chorus)
Input Impedance	
(Input, Effect Receive)	500 K ohms
Output Impedance	
(Outputs 1 & 2, Eff Send)	<1K ohms
Dimensions	310(w) x 190(d) x 70(h)mm
Weight	2.1 kg, 4.6 lbs.
Power Requirements	120 VAC, 60 Hz, 6W
	220 – 240 VAC, 50 Hz 8W

UE305 FLOOR SYSTEM

The UE305 Floor System contains three popular signal processors for keyboards, guitars or bass. The Compressor/Limiter with variable attack time, the Analog Delay for quality echo and hand reverb effects, and the Stereo Chorus for a swirling multi-dimensional sound. The stereo output enhances all of the effects of the UE305. A third output is provided for echo "ping-pong" effects or for system branching. An external loop between the Compressor/Limiter and Analog Delay allow the control of additional signal processors. The Q-1 switching system is used for silent switching of each section and master control. The UE305—another reason why Ibanez leads the way in signal processing.

SPECIFICATIONS

Comp/Limit Compression Ratio	40dB
Analog Delay Range	10 – 300 ms
Stereo Chorus Delay Range	3.2 – 8.5 ms
Input Impedance	
(Input, Effect Receive)	500K ohms
Output Impedance	
(Outputs 1, 2, 3 and effect send)	<1K ohms
Dimensions	310(w) x 190(d) x 70(h)mm
Weight	2.1 kg, 4.6 lbs
Power Requirements	120 VAC, 60 Hz, 5W
	220 – 240 VAC, 50 Hz, 7W

Ibanez by the Numbers

A 1979 Ibanez catalog shows the following compact effects: FL-303 and FL-305 Flangers, PT-707 and PT-909 Phase Shifters, OD-850 and OD-855 Overdrives, CP-830 Compressor, and model 93 Blubber wah-wah. Also introduced were the AD-220 Analog Delay with Multi-Flanger, AD-3000 Analog Delay with Multi-Flanger, AD-150 Analog Delay, UE-700 Multi-Effects Rack, GE-500 and GE-1000 graphic equalizers, and GE-300 Power Equalizer.

Ibanez's 1980 pedal lineup included the GE-601 Graphic Equalizer, CP-835 Compressor, AD-80 Analog Delay, FL-301 Flanger, TS-808 Tube Screamer, CS-505 Stereo Chorus, and PT-909 Phase Tone.

In 1981 Ibanez added a few new units and dropped the hyphens in model numbers.

Ibanez boxes linked via "crank" connectors

Offerings included the AD80 Analog Delay, AF201 Auto Filter, CP835 Compressor, CS505 Stereo Chorus, FL301 Flanger, GE601 Graphic EQ, PQ401 Parametric EQ, PT909 Phase Tone, TS808, and AD100 Analog Delay.

Model names changed again in '82 with the PT9 Phaser, FL9 Flanger, CS9 Stereo Chorus, TS9 Tube Screamer, SD9 Sonic Distortion, CP9 Compressor/ Limiter, AD9 Stereo Analog Delay, GE9 6-Band Graphic EQ, PQ9 Parametric EQ, and AF9 Auto Filter. New offerings for '83 included the AD100 Compact Analog Delay, AD202 Multi-Mode Analog Delay, Blubber wah-wah and Double Sound distortion/wah pedals, the rack-mount UE400 and UE405 analog multi-effects processors and the UE300, UE305, and UE303B floor-mounted multi-effectors.

During this period Ibanez also introduced the DM1000 Digital Delay and HD1000 Harmonics/Delay rackmount processors. These were followed by DMD2000 Programmable Digital Delay and HD1500 Programmable Harmonics/Delay. Digital pedals such as the DDL 10 Delay II, DCF 10 Chorus/ Flanger, and the DML 10 Modulation Delay II were also offered. In 1988 Ibanez introduced the PDD1 Delay, PDM1 Modulation Delay, and PDS1 Distortion pedals. These programmable stomp-boxes featured tiny LCD displays and push-button keys, ten factory preset sounds, and nine user memory locations.

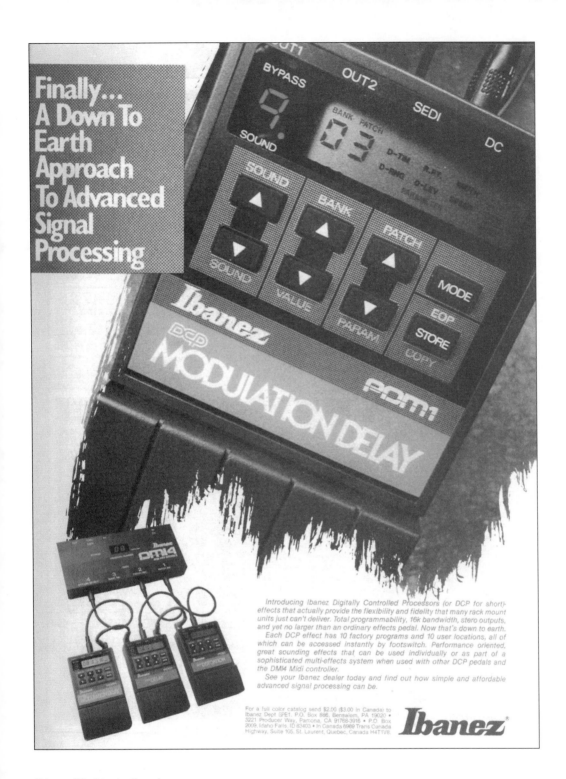

*February '88 ad touting Ibanez's
programmable DCP series.*

83

MAESTRO

One of the companies most responsible for the effects explosion of the mid '60s to late '70s was Maestro, a subsidiary of Chicago Musical Instruments, which also owned Gibson. The Maestro saga began in 1963 with the introduction of the Maestro Fuzz-Tone. After the Rolling Stones' '65 hit "Satisfaction," the box became so popular that CMI had to enlist other divisions, such as Lowry Organ, as well as outside subcontractors to make Fuzz-Tones.

Oberheim's first product for Maestro was the ring modulator.

HERE COMES THE FUZZ!

The Maestro Fuzz-Tone can make your guitar sound like a buzz-saw. It purrs, growls or bites . . . depending on how you treat it. Just plug your instrument into the Fuzz-Tone and operate the foot switch button with the tap of your foot. Tap on the switch once for fuzz-tone effects. Tap again to bring back natural guitar amplification.

There's an 'Attack' control that enables you to increase fuzz distortion. You can go from a very faint fuzz that'll remind you of a painless drill, to a hefty, biting fuzz that you'd swear could cut down trees.

Maestro also features a Fuzz-Tone 'Volume' control. Turn it clockwise and really come on strong.

Visit your Maestro dealer and ask for a demonstration. The Fuzz-Tone is waiting to join your group . . . so step on it!

FEATURES and SPECIFICATIONS
Controls — On/Off Volume; Attack; Foot-Switch On/Off.

MAESTRO DIVISION, CHICAGO MUSICAL INSTRUMENT CO., 7373 N. CICERO AVE., LINCOLNWOOD, ILL. 60646

Late '60s Fuzz-Tone ad.

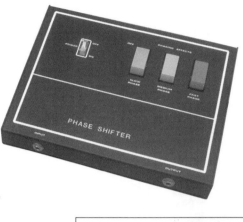

*The Tom Oberheim-
designed Phase Shifter and
his original prototype.*

PHASE SHIFTER

*Rover rotating speaker above an
assortment of Maestro pedals.*

CMI was purchased by Norlin in '69, and two years later, Norlin president Les Prop hired Bob Rubin—a buyer who had overseen the impressive growth of Montgomery Ward's musical-instrument sales—to consolidate all of Norlin's effects (including the famed Echoplex) under the Maestro banner.

Rubin enlisted the aid of computer engineer Tom Oberheim, who subsequently designed Maestro's first phase shifter, and Richard Mintz, who was a production manager at Fairchild Camera before founding Long Island's All-Test Devices in 1970. Mintz and his partner—both of whom were musicians—built guitar effects on the side and occasionally sold them through Manny's in New York. One of their first products was a sustainer designed for Leslie West. Through Manny's, Mintz hooked up with CMI, which asked him to redesign its wah-wah pedal. The result was the circa-'70 Maestro Boomerang wah/volume pedal.

Early '70s Maestro ad.

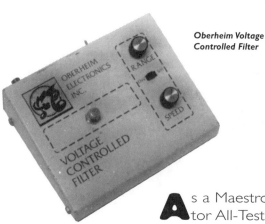

Oberheim Voltage Controlled Filter

As a Maestro subcontractor All-Test made the Fuzz-Tone, SS-2 Sustainer, and Boomerang, as well as the Maestro Super Fuzz, Octave Box, Bass Brassmaster, Full Range Booster, Envelope Modifier and Multiplier, and a line of acoustic-guitar transducers.

A circa-'72 Maestro catalog shows these effects and devices: Octave Box, Theramin, Super Fuzz, Sustainer, Bass Brassmaster, Envelope Modifier, Phase Shifter, Fuzz Phazzer, Wah Wah Volume Pedal, Boomerang, Echoplex, Echoplex Groupmaster, Rover, Maestro Rhythm King, Sireko By Echoplex, Ring Modulator, Rhythm 'N' Sound, Woodwind Sound System, and Rhythm Queen. In 1975 ATD began marketing pickup systems, preamps, EQs, mixers, and pedals

under their own name. A 1976 ATD catalog also shows two pedals—the EV-1 volume and the WV-1 wah/volume.

By 1976 Maestro had new management, and their effects received a big makeover. Moog Electronics of Buffalo, New York, now manufactured most of the devices, including a highly original series of rounded-wedge-shaped boxes that featured large foot-actuated control wheels on either side. These TFC (total foot control) products included the MP-1 Phaser, MPP-1 Stage Phaser, MFZ-1 Fuzz, MFZT-1 Fuzztain, and MPF-1 Parametric Filter. This final series remained in production until Maestro threw in the towel in 1978. In 1975 Tom Oberheim began making polyphonic synthesizers under his own name. He sold Oberheim in '85 (the name was changed to ECC Developments), and in '87 started his current synth company, Marion Systems Corporation.

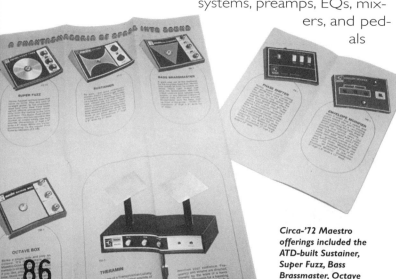

Circa-'72 Maestro offerings included the ATD-built Sustainer, Super Fuzz, Bass Brassmaster, Octave Box, and Envelope Modifier.

STEP ON THE WILD SIDE
WITH BOOMERANG

Boomerang is the sound effects volume/wow-wow pedal that turns a conservative performance into a gassy gig. It connects between your instrument and amplifier, and is controlled by the tap of your foot.

Step on the Boomerang firmly and it's a volume expression pedal. The amount of volume can be controlled by the pedal position. Depress the pedal all the way for a sound that's ferociously strong. Let up on the pedal, and the sound becomes a meek, little whisper.

When it's time to add effects, depress the pedal firmly again, and you'll activate the switch that turns on the wow-wow.

Depending on how the expression pedal is controlled, you can achieve anything from a speedy, weird space sound to a slow, moaning, groaning sound. Unlimited versatility!

Boomerang works on electric guitars, portable organs, Maestro sound systems . . . almost anything amplified. Visit your Maestro dealer and ask for a demonstration. The Boomerang is waiting to join your group . . . so step on it!

FEATURES and SPECIFICATIONS

MAESTRO "Boomerang" Pedal, Model BG-2. A battery operated, completely transistorized volume/wow control pedal. Dimensions: 3" high x 12" long x 5" wide. Weight: 3 lbs.

INPUT JACK
One for instrument. (This is also the Power On-Off switch.)

OUTPUT JACK
One for amplifier.

STANDARD EQUIPMENT
The following accessories are included with every "Boomerang" pedal.

> 1 Output Cord
> (Fits any standard amp jack.)
> 1 Carrying Case

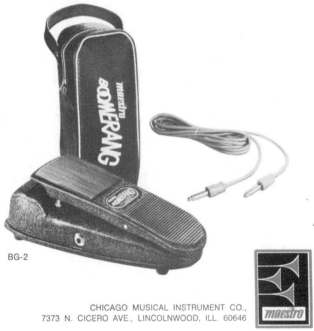

BG-2

CHICAGO MUSICAL INSTRUMENT CO.,
7373 N. CICERO AVE., LINCOLNWOOD, ILL. 60646

The ATD-designed Boomerang.

LET YOUR FOOT LEND A HAND

Tom Oberheim's Story

I had decided to try to make some kind of a phasing or flanging circuit in the late '60s, but back then I really didn't know the difference between the two. I got a Leslie speaker and experimented with it, but with my limited knowledge and lack of proper test equipment I couldn't really figure out what was going on.

That led me to investigate flanging because I thought there might be some similarity between flanging and what a Leslie does.

I went to a guy named Paul Beaver—one of the pioneers of electronic music in the Los Angeles area in the '50s and '60s—and he explained to me how tape-recorder flanging worked. The key to that, of course, is mixing a time-delayed signal with the original signal, which causes some notches in the frequency response. When you move the notches around, you get this swooshing sound. In 1970 I wasn't aware of any time delay circuits, so I found a phase shifter circuit in a book and tried that. It worked well enough, so I started making the PS-1 Phase Shifter.

About the time I put the PS-1 on the market, I came across another phase

shifter being made by a guy named Carl Countryman. It was more of a studio thing, however, because it didn't have a modulation oscillator, just a big dial that you turned to change the phase. The Uni-Vibe was on the market when I brought out the Phase Shifter, but it certainly wasn't making much of an impact. As far as I know, I had the first solid-state phase shifter that was designed for performing musicians.

My first product wasn't the PS-1, but rather a ring modulator. That's what led to my contact with CMI/Norlin. They saw my ring modulator somewhere, called up and worked out a deal with me, and we started selling them. After I developed the Phase Shifter, I took one to [Maestro's] Bob Rubin, who made the comment, "Well, it doesn't do much, but maybe we can sell a few."

The Moog-made Maestros sported large foot-activated wheels.

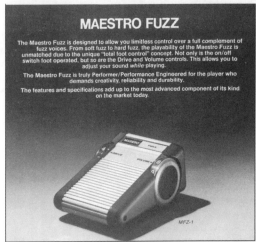

MAESTRO FUZZ

The Maestro Fuzz is designed to allow you limitless control over a full complement of fuzz voices. From soft fuzz to hard fuzz, the playability of the Maestro Fuzz is unmatched due to the unique "total foot control" concept. Not only is the on/off switch foot operated, but so are the Drive and Volume controls. This allows you to adjust your sound *while* playing.

The Maestro Fuzz is truly Performer/Performance Engineered for the player who demands creativity, reliability and durability.

The features and specifications add up to the most advanced component of its kind on the market today.

MFZ-1

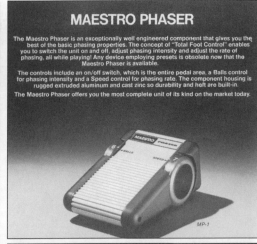

MAESTRO PHASER

The Maestro Phaser is an exceptionally well engineered component that gives you the best of the basic phasing properties. The concept of "Total Foot Control" enables you to switch the unit on and off, adjust phasing intensity and adjust the rate of phasing, all while playing! Any device employing presets is obsolete now that the Maestro Phaser is available.

The controls include an on/off switch, which is the entire pedal area, a Balls control for phasing intensity and a Speed control for phasing rate. The component housing is rugged extruded aluminum and cast zinc so durability and heft are built-in.

The Maestro Phaser offers you the most complete unit of its kind on the market today.

MP-1

MAESTRO FUZZTAIN

The Maestro Fuzztain is a superbly designed component specifically engineered to give you unlimited control over a full range of fuzz voices plus a sustain that makes each note last a long, long time with all its full, rich, original tone quality.

Besides unequaled sounds, the Maestro Fuzztain can be played as no other device on the market due to its "total foot control" concept. The on/off switch, drive control for adjusting fuzz and sustain intensity, volume control, and rotary foot switch for selecting soft fuzz, hard fuzz or sustain, are all controlled by the foot. This means you can adjust the Maestro Fuzztain while playing.

The Maestro Fuzztain is also a very rugged, reliable component. It will be considered the most advanced, most complete component of its kind on the market.

MFZT-1

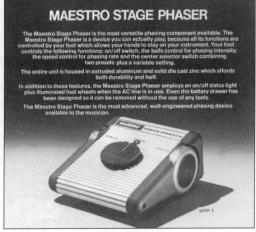

MAESTRO STAGE PHASER

The Maestro Stage Phaser is the most versatile phasing component available. The Maestro Stage Phaser is a device you can actually *play*, because all its functions are controlled by your foot which allows your hands to stay on your instrument. Your foot controls the following functions: on/off switch, the balls control for phasing intensity, the speed control for phasing rate and the center selector switch containing two presets plus a variable setting.

The entire unit is housed in extruded aluminum and solid die cast zinc which affords both durability and heft.

In addition to these features, the Maestro Stage Phaser employs an on/off status light plus illuminated foot wheels when the AC line is in use. Even the battery drawer has been designed so it can be removed without the use of any tools.

The Maestro Stage Phaser is the most advanced, well-engineered phasing device available to the musician.

MPP-1

Between '71 and '75 my little company built and sold around 30,000 to 40,000 PS-1s to Maestro. My price to Norlin was $47 per unit. I wasn't a very good businessman back then, and there was no foot pedal market, but the Phase Shifter really put me in business. I remember one month my sales totaled $150,000, and the company was just me and one other person! Even though I'd started out trying to electronically mimic a rotating speaker, the Phase Shifter really became its own thing.

The PS-1 soon became an anachronism, however, because it had those silly Lowry switches and a circuit that was designed to change speeds slowly—like a real rotating speaker does—when you shifted from slow to fast or vice versa. It quickly got to the point where that feature just wasn't important to most people.

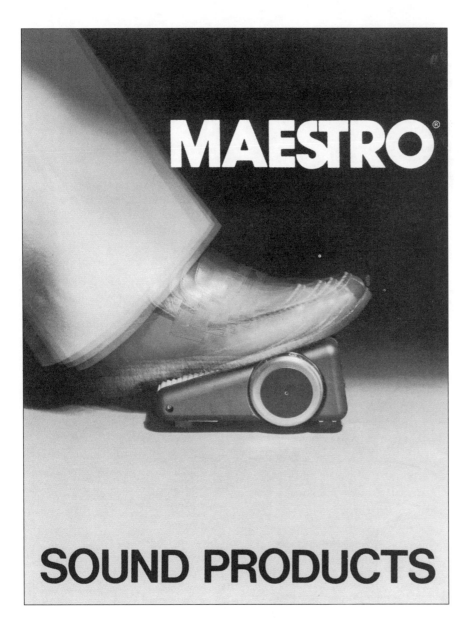

MAESTRO®

SOUND PRODUCTS

The only other thing I had was the USS-1, or Universal Synthesizer System-1. That was a preamp and distortion circuit designed by my first engineer, who later started a company called JL Cooper. It also had a phase shifter and voltage-controlled filter with a triggered envelope. It was a big black thing with bright red, yellow and blue paint on it. The PS-1 board was also put in some Standel guitar amps.

My relationship with Maestro lasted until January 25, 1975. That was the day they called and canceled all their orders because Norlin was in financial trouble. By that time the PS-1 was obsolete, but I'd been selling a smaller phase shifter to Norlin called the Mini Phase and a voltage-controlled filter called the Filter Sample Hold. After Norlin, I repainted those units off-white with black lettering, and sold them as Oberheim products.

ROGER MAYER

Among effects frontiersmen, Roger Mayer stands as tall as Davy Crockett and Daniel Boone. The British-born stompbox designer's first electronics gig was with the Royal Navy, but in the early '60s he began building fuzzes for local hotshots such as Jimmy Page and Jeff Beck. Mayer claims his original fuzz is heard on Beck's work in early Yardbirds hits such as "Heart Full of Soul," "Over Under Sideways Down," and "Shapes of Things." Page, who played briefly with Beck in the Yardbirds and then succeeded him, remembers Beck's having a Mayer pedal.

In 1966 Mayer met Hendrix and showed him his newest creation, the Octavia. Roger later took the device to Olympic recording studios, where Jimi used its unique second-octave fuzz effect on "Purple Haze" and "Fire." Mayer says that over the next few years he built dozens of effects for Hendrix, including the Axis fuzz, which Jimi used for his solo on "Bold as Love."

Mayer also helped equip Jimi's Electric Lady studios in New York, which gave Roger the opportunity to work with Stevie Wonder and Malcolm Cecil during the recording of *Innervisions* and *Music of My Mind*. Other Mayer clients have included the Isley Brothers, Junior Marvin, and Bob Marley.

Mayer returned to Surrey in 1988, where he now produces a line of effects that includes the Octavia, Classic Fuzz, Axis Fuzz, Mongoose Fuzz, Voodoo-1, VooDoo Bass, and Vision Wah. Roger also makes the 9090A Wah Electronic Kit, which fits into the Dunlop CryBaby housing and offers up 16 sweep settings.

Roger Mayer's Story

I was born in Surrey, England, and got my electronics education through the Royal Naval Scientific Service. They sent me to a university for five years, where I got laboratory and scientific training, plus a regular education. That taught me a lot about solving problems in interesting ways.

The first time I ever heard a fuzz was on a Ventures song called "2,000 Pound Bumblebee." It was an interesting sound, but there were no fuzzboxes in England at that time. I got around to making one for a local guitarist named Jimmy Page, and he used it on some of his early recordings. Then I made one for his friend Big Jim Sullivan, who had gotten Jimmy into the session business. At the time Big Jim was one of the leading session players. He used my fuzz on one of the first hit records in England to feature fuzz, P.J. Proby's "Hold Me," in 1964. After that I became interested in the various kinds of distortion, because there's obviously more to a fuzzbox than simply squaring off a wave.

During that time I was working in vibration acoustical analysis and warfare stuff, and my first boxes were just simple transistor amplifiers. In 1964 we were using germanium transistors because the silicon types were not yet widely available. We had some military versions, but they cost about the equivalent of a week's wages.

One the most important aspects of any distortion box is the way it decays. If it doesn't have a perfectly smooth decay or it makes noise between the notes, it sounds like shit. The guitar you're using and the type of EQ that's applied before or

Mayer Octavia, Classic Fuzz, Axis fuzz, Mongoose Fuzz, and Voodoo 1 attack an invading Vox CryBaby.

after the distortion also makes a big difference. If you increase the output of the box too much, it blows up the amp's front end, which may or may not have a desirable effect. If you're using germanium transistors—which have a very round, soft sound—you've got to play with the output level that you're going to hit the amp with until you find the sweet spot. There's quite a lot of experimentation involved. The equalization before the distortion is also very important because the distortion always adds upper harmonics.

I never particularly cared for the Vox Tone Bender's sound, and the Fuzz Face circuit is straight out of any early electronics book. It's a minimum-parts-count circuit, and it has a lot of design drawbacks. Very few Fuzz Faces sounded any good, and when they started being made with silicon transistors, they were fucking nightmares. They picked up radio and

93

Hendrix with an early Mayer Octavia.
Photo: Joseph Sia

modulator with some things to add more harmonics. The Octavia doubles the frequency and provides almost a mirror image of the sound, and it's dynamically responsive to some degree. A few people have ripped me off on the Octavia. One was Tychobrahe. They made a few, but it didn't go anywhere.

When Jimi first heard the Octavia, he loved it. Within a few days we went into the studio, and he took the original recording of "Purple Haze"—which didn't have a solo on it—and added the Octavia in an overdub. That really made the definitive sound at the end of the record. At the same session he did the solo on "Fire."

The Octavia was originally voiced for a Strat, and on "One Rainy Wish" [*Axis: Bold as Love*] we would often use the neck pickup with bass added in order to get rid of some of the harmonics from the strings. That let us double a purer tone and made it sound a bit more flute-like. The signal chain was quite complicated on that album because we had a Sound City amp, a Marshall, and a direct sound. On "Purple Haze" and "Fire," Jimi went straight into a Marshall.

had all kinds of problems. When I was with Jimi I designed the Axis Fuzz, which had a completely different configuration than the Fuzz Face. It was much more stable and smooth sounding, and it didn't pick up radio. You can hear that sound on "Bold as Love." It's definitely not a Fuzz Face.

The first time I saw Jimi, he was using a Fuzz Face. Then when he did "Purple Haze," he used my Octavia and a Fuzz Face. After that I started playing with Fuzz Faces—selecting them out, messing with the EQ, and stuff like that. The Octavia had been an idea that I'd discussed with Page before I met Hendrix. It's like a ring

I took a leave of absence from the Admiralty in early '68 in order to join Jimi on his American tour. I wasn't a member of the crew or anything like that; I just traveled with the band. It was just his way of saying thanks for helping him on *Axis*. I used to spend a lot of time privately with Jimi as a friend and hanging out with him and Kathy [Etchingham-Page] at their flat, just playing around with sounds. Jimi and I were both very fast at absorbing different sounds and figuring out what could be done. A lot of the things I did for him were customized for the song. A little difference in EQ can make a big difference in the sound.

Eventually I moved to America, married an American girl, and started building studio consoles and recording equipment. I was involved with three Stevie Wonder albums at Electric Lady studios, where I built part of the analog synthesizer that was used on "Superstition." Then I met the Isley Brothers. I did all of Ernie's stuff after Jimi died. I was working with quite a few of the guitar players in New York, but I was primarily making recording-studio stuff like limiters, EQs, and compressors. I sold that stuff to Atlantic Records, The Record Plant, and The Hit Factory.

After I came back to England, I took some time off and then went to work at Olympic Studios in London, where I designed some of the mixing consoles. It was a better-paying job than the Admiralty, and bit more interesting too. I had been promoted at a very young age and would have had to wait until I was 27 to get my next promotion. The job was going nowhere fast. If you're good at what you do, once you get promoted you've got to wait for dead men's shoes. I also went to the Barbados for a couple of years and started a factory there. When I got back to England, the demand for effects pedals had really increased.

I designed the rocket-shaped enclosure for the Octavia in 1980, and then we started putting other things into it. It's a very attractive housing, and kind of a logo too. When it's on the bloody floor you take one look at it and you know it's mine. You can drop it and it can't fall on the knobs, and you can hit the footswitch from any angle. We use that box for the Octavia, Classic Fuzz, Axis Fuzz and the Mongoose. I came out with the Mongoose because someone told me that the Pro Co Rat pedal sounded quite good but was a bit noisy. I had a listen, and then, without copying the Rat, I made something similar that sounded better. I have a history of listening to what people like.

MORLEY

With their photo-resistor circuitry that made noisy potentiometers seem utterly Stone Age, Morley's big, chrome-plated AC-powered pedals were the battleships of the '70s stompbox scene. Tel-Ray Electronics of Burbank, California, entered the effects game in the late '60s with a series of wah, boost, fuzz, and Leslie-simulation pedals. Founding brothers Marvin and Raymond Lubow must have been quite proud of their rotating-sound technology, because "Morley" originated as a play on the Leslie name: more lee instead of less lee.

Morley's first offerings included the Power Wah Boost, Power Wah Fuzz, Rotating Sound Power Wah Expression Pedal, and the Rotating Sound Synthesizer. During the early '70s Morley sold their Ad-N-Echo memory system to Fender and Thomas Organ, and by the end of the decade were also distributing Moonstone guitars.

The EVO-1 Echo Volume: A huge, eight-pound monster that stored sounds electrostatically on a spinning disk.

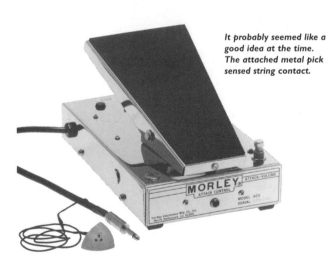

It probably seemed like a good idea at the time. The attached metal pick sensed string contact.

The battery- or AC-powered Compact series measured a mere 6 5/8" X 4" X 2 5/8".

MORLEY™

MUSICAL PRODUCTS

"More Sounds of Tomorrow"

The Morley Man's evolution from mellow tallguy to odious '70s rocker.

MORLEY MEN DO IT...

...with their feet

The select-Effect allowed five effects to be controlled by one foot.

Morley's Slimline series could operate on battery or AC power.

circa '81 noise gate/line driver.

By the early '80s Morley's greatly expanded product line included the Power Wah (PWO), Volume (VOL), Wah/Volume (WVO), Volume Boost (VBO), Stereo Volume (SVO), Pro Phaser (PFA), Automatic Wah (PWA), Volume Phaser (PFV), Rotating Wah (RWV), Pro Panner (PVL), Power Wah Fuzz (PWF), Power Wah Boost (PWB), Echo Volume (EVO-1), Stereo Chorus Flanger (CFL), Volume Compressor (VCO), Electrostatic Delay Line (EDL), Bigfoot Power Amp (an 8-pound amp-in-a-pedal that could drive speakers with its 25-watt output

stage), and a device called the Select-Effect that used a sideways-motion pedal to select among five different effects. During this period Morley also introduced the Analog Echo Reverb, Echo Chorus Vibrato, 747 Milli-Second Delay, and the battery-powered Slimline pedals.

Later the company stretched out even further with the Amp Output Control, a volume pedal that accepted amplifier outputs as high as 200 watts and provided panning control for two speakers. The Electro-Pik series pedals (Electro-Pik-Percussion, Electro-Pik-Attack, and Electro-Pik-A-Wah) sported electrically attached

POWER WAH (PWO)

WAH/VOLUME (WVO)

STEREO VOLUME (SVO)

VOLUME (VOL)

VOLUME/BOOST (VBO)

PRO PHASER (PFA)

POWER WAH FUZZ (PWF)

POWER WAH/BOOST (PWB)

PRO PANNER (PVL)

Seen one, seen 'em all: Morley's mid-'70s line-up.

ECHO/VOLUME (EVO-1)

The exclusive and patented Morley Echo system is non-magnetic. Because no tapes or magnetic discs are used the hiss noise and routine servicing associated with tape systems are eliminated. Studio quality signal to noise ratio plus wide range response from 30Hz up, make the EVO ideal for vocalists and for use with any musical instrument. The pedal provides continuously variable control of repeats from a single repeat to multiples to runaway or instant cancel. Dual output jacks are provided for true stereo operation with a foot switch to combine both channels for mono. Two master controls allow total regulation of Echo Volume and the maximum number of repeats. A continuously variable delay control offers precise adjustment of the time between records. A second foot switch turns the Echo off and permits the treadle to be used as a Volume/Expression Pedal. No other echo, regardless of cost, can match the performance of the Morley Echo/Volume Pedal.

We build it failsafe because your career depends on it — and so does ours.

(EVO-1)

AUTOMATIC WAH (PWA)

VOLUME PHASER (PFV)

ROTATING WAH (RWV)

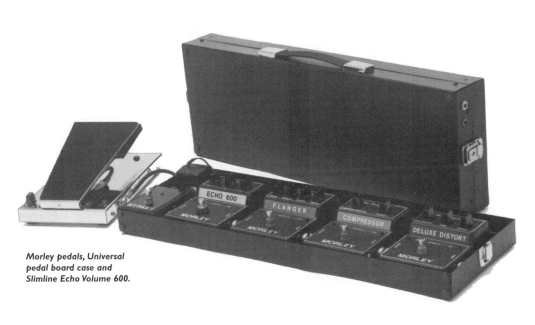

Morley pedals, Universal pedal board case and Slimline Echo Volume 600.

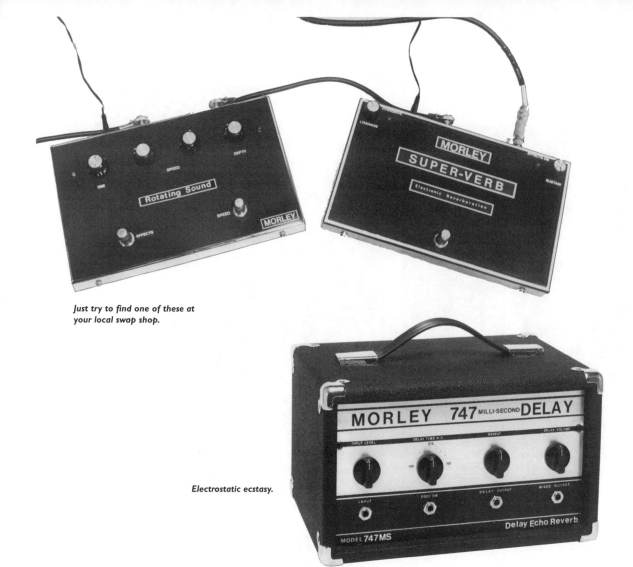

*Just try to find one of these at
your local swap shop.*

Electrostatic ecstasy.

metal picks that sensed when contact was made or broken with the strings, and the Sync-Attack and Sync-A-Wah boxes clipped onto the guitar strap and provided either bowed-instrument or auto-wah effects.

Morley also introduced several non-pedal stompboxes, including the Pro Compressor, Phaser One, Stereo Chorus Vibrato, Deluxe Distortion, Analog Echo Reverb, Deluxe Phaser, Noise Gate/Line Driver, Deluxe Flanger, and Distortion One.

The Lubow brothers sold Morley to Accutronics (a division of the Marmon Group) in January 1989. Now called Sound Enhancements, this part of the Accutronics company continues to produce Morley effects.

MOSRITE

Semie Moseley's strange and wonderful electric guitars were used in the '50s and '60s by artists such as Merle Travis, Little Jimmy Dickens, Lefty Frizzell, Joe Maphis, Larry Collins, and the Ventures' Nokie Edwards. Besides being a talented guitar builder, Semie was a restless evangelical Christian musician who moved his company (when it was in business) from Los Angeles

Semie Moseley.

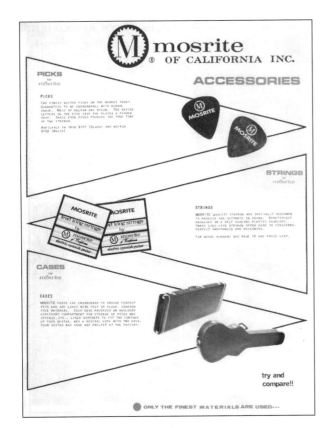

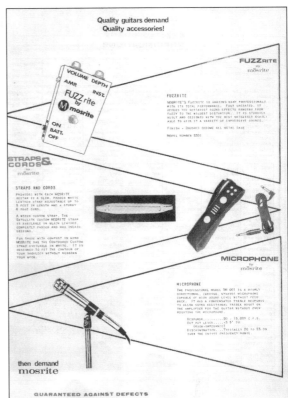

to Bakersfield, California, then to Carson City, Nevada, and finally to Jonas Ridge, North Carolina.

During a high point in the late '60s, Mosrite introduced the Fuzzrite fuzz. Designed by Mosrite electronics technician Eddie Sanner, the Fuzzrite featured a brushed-chrome metal case, volume and depth controls, and a side-mounted battery switch. Eddie still lives in Bakersfield, where he builds solid-state amps for guitar and pedal steel. Semie Moseley died in 1992.

Eddie Sanner's Story

I started working for Semie Moseley in 1960, first on guitars, and then guitar electronics. The Maestro Fuzz-Tone was becoming extremely popular in the early '60s, and Semie asked me to come up with a similar circuit Mosrite could produce. The result was a box that I named the Fuzzrite. We introduced it in 1966. The first 250 Fuzzrites used germanium transistors, but when I discovered that they wouldn't fuzz properly when set on cold concrete, we switched to silicon transistors. They were much more stable.

The Fuzzrite turned out to be a big seller. During our peak we were shipping 1,000 units a month. Since Semie made a $10 profit on each one, it wasn't long before he was driving a brand-new Cadillac. It didn't last long, though. Semie started having major cash-flow

Even church ladies dug Mosrites.

problems that were caused mainly by a crooked parts guy who was getting kick-backs for over-ordering certain components.

I remember trying to build the Fuzzrites, and we'd run out of something. I'd go to the parts area and find jillions of some things and zero of others. Of course, Semie had other problems as well. After I quit in '69, he and his family stayed afloat making Fuzzrites in their kitchen. They continued making them into the '70s.

After Mosrite, I went to work for Rosac, which was an electronics offshoot of the Sierra Bag Company. Rosac stood for Rosenberg and Sacco, the last names of the two owners. I designed the Nu Fuzz, Distortion Blender, Tremolo, and Nu Wa pedals for Rosac, as well as a line of P.A. gear. The boxes were influenced by other units I'd heard—including the Fuzzrite—but I've never liked the idea of copying other people's designs. I've always tried to make each of my circuits as original as possible.

SOLID STATE AMPLIFIERS

QUALITY ENGINEERED BY

CONSTANT RESEARCH FROM MOSRITE ELECTRONICS PRO-
DUCED THESE QUALITY FEATURES:

* FULLY TRANSISTORIZED
* SILICONE SEMI-CONDUCTORS
* ADVANCED SOLID STATE CIRCUITS
* ACCURATELY CONTROLLED FUZZRITE
* BRIGHT, FULL SOUNDING REVERB
* SMOOTH, QUICK, RESPONSIVE TREMELO
* SPECIAL DESIGNED 15 INCH HEAVY DUTY JENSEN
  SPEAKERS WITH OPTIONAL 15 INCH ALTEC
  LANSING SPEAKERS
* ACOUSTICAL ENGINEERED, ENCLOSED CABINET
* SKUFF RESISTANT BLACK TOLEX COVERING

EXPERT ENGINEERING
DURABILITY
BEAUTY

MOSRITE SOLID STATE AMPLIFIERS ARE AVAIL-
ABLE IN THREE OUTSTANDING MODELS.
FOR SPECIFICATIONS OF EACH SEE PAGE 16.

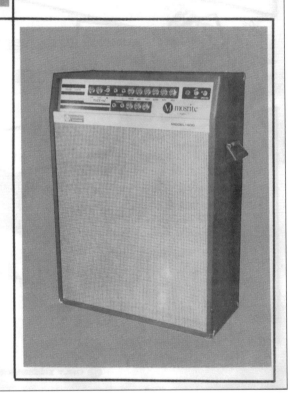

Mosrite made amps too.

Aged cheese: An extremely moldy Fuzzrite.

Rosac's Sanner-designed Nu Wa.

Early stompboxes were often cheaply made and unreliable, but MXR changed all that with their superbly crafted effects line. MXR was founded by teenage entrepreneurs Terry Sherwood and Keith Barr, who had met at Rush Henrietta High School in Rochester, New York. In 1971 Barr and Sherwood opened an audio-repair business called Audio Services. Besides working on stereos, they also fixed fuzzboxes and other pedals for local musicians.

After seeing the problems players encountered with their stompboxes, Keith and Terry determined they could do better. In 1972 they formed MXR and began producing the Phase 90, their first design, in the basement of their rented home. The neat little orange phaser was an instant hit. Starting with an initial production run of 50 units, MXR grew rapidly through the '70s and early '80s, eventually becoming a multi-million-dollar company with over 170 employees.

Among MXR's best-known pedals were the Analog Delay, Blue Box, Distortion Plus, Dynacomp, Flanger, Graphic EQ, Noise-Gate Line Driver, Phase 45, Phase 90, Phase 100, and Stereo Chorus. The company was also one of the prime movers in analog and digital rackmount effects.

It would be tough to find a major artist who hasn't plugged into an MXR box. Eddie Van Halen said he used an MXR Flanger and favored the Phase 90's treble boost for solos. Keith Richards got his classic sound on "Shattered" and "Beast of Burden" using a Phase 100, and he also reported using an Analog Delay and a Graphic EQ live. Jerry Garcia was a Distortion Plus fan, and Aerosmith's Joe Perry once said, "I have a compressor, an equalizer, a phaser, and a flanger—it's all MXR stuff." Peter Frampton described setting up a Foxx fuzztone with an MXR Analog Delay and a Stereo Chorus—all in one box: "When I press one button, all of them come on at the same time, and the sound is really quite unique. I used that on 'Dig What I Say.'"

Jim Dunlop is now re-creating such MXR hits as the Distortion Plus, Blue Box, Dynacomp, Phase 90, Phase 100, 6-Band Graphic EQ, and Micro Amp. Keith Barr, who went on to form Alesis, and former chief engineer Richard Neatrour, who helped start Applied Research & Technology, provided these reminiscences of the MXR years.

Keith Barr's Story

My father was a physicist, and he taught me a lot of stuff when I was a kid. I thought I was pretty smart, so I quit school when I was 17 and moved out to California, where I got a job in aerospace designing the electronics for gyroscopes. Around 1970 there were some layoffs that made me afraid that I wouldn't be able to find continued employment. I contacted one of my high school buddies, Terry Sherwood, and we decided to return to New York, move in with our folks and start an audio repair shop. We were kids and we didn't know any better. We had a great time fixing stereos for people in the neighborhood. Of course, guitar players always had equipment that was failing, and we started fixing that too.

I played guitar when I was a kid, and I loved making amplifiers and little widgets, so when I saw the poor quality of the effects devices that were coming in for repair, I was really amazed. Eager to start designing some things, I made up a few little boxes for my guitar-playing friends. They seemed to like them.

Terry and I were also doing some sound reinforcement. There was a com-

pany called Brighton Sound who were like our big brothers. We were trying to learn from them. One day I was working on design for a mixer that I thought might have commercial value, and one of our friends came in and said, "You ought to call your company MXR, for mixer." I didn't think it was a bad idea, but I liked the idea of adding things to a concept, so I dubbed it MXR Innovations.

We made one mixer, but I didn't much care about it because I was much more interested in phase shifters. I knew about the Tom Oberheim-designed phaser that Maestro was distributing, but I refused to look at it when one came into our shop for repair. It was very important to me that I didn't copy anybody.

I was about eight when I first encountered phase-shifting in the Radio Amateur's Handbook. It was an all-pass circuit section designed to notch out interference from radio receivers, but several of these sections chained together make a phase shifter for music.

The whole concept of phase-shifting is very close to flanging, which used to really catch our fancy. You took a pair of tape recorders playing the same thing, and then synchronized them to give this wonderful flanging sound. We used to imagine what kind of frequency

New building, new logo.

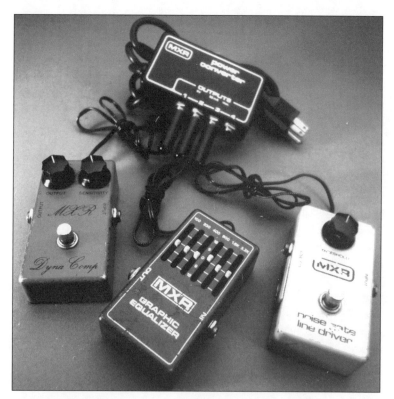

Dyna Comp, Graphic Equalizer, and Noise Gate Line Driver with Power Converter.

the second-harmonic distortion that pours out of a Phase 90 has a hell of a lot do to with how it sounds—especially with guitar.

When we were ready to start producing the Phase 90, we took $500 out of the cash drawer—probably all the money we had—to buy stuff to make them. We bought the die-cast boxes from a company called Bud, but we still had to have them painted and silkscreened. We bought a spray-painting kit from Sears for about $40 and set up a little paint booth with an old exhaust fan somebody had given us in the basement of a house that Terry and I rented.

Our boxes were painted an orange color that I saw on the road one day. It was a particularly stunning shade that Ford offered on their Econoline van. We didn't know how to dry it, so the first couple hundred Phase 90s dried hanging from our clothesline in the backyard. There were even bugs stuck to some of those early units.

We built our own silkscreens too. My father had a photo lab, and we did all the photo preparation there, including the script logo that I came up with. I'd been turned on to graphics when I was living in Venice, California, by a group who called themselves the Los Angeles Fine Art Squad. They were a bunch of artists from UCLA who did a lot of murals in the late '60s. The

response we were listening to, and it was pretty obvious that this phasing notch-filter circuit would cause that to happen.

Guitarists would come into our shop and tell us that the phase-shifting thing was really happening, so I built one and people said they liked it. The Phase 90 produced two notches in the frequency spectrum, and it swept them up and down a range of midrange frequencies at a rate determined by the rate control. The location of those notches in the audio band and the sweep width is the key to how you perceive the effect. The Phase 90 achieved its notch-position variation through the use of FETs, which is a type of transistor that has the ability to act like a resistor whose value can be controlled by a voltage. They also distort, and concept of packaging the units in heavy cardboard boxes with foam strips around the inside came from a guy I used to hang with who was into construction using unusual materials.

We even silkscreened our own circuit boards and etched them in a fish tank. At first we'd go to companies that made boards and ask for their scraps. I personally drilled the first couple thousand Phase 90 circuit boards with a drill press my dad gave us. We also employed teenagers to work for minimum wage in terrible conditions in our basement.

Things really got going when we met a guy at the local radio supply store named Mike Laiacona, who now runs Whirlwind. He was young punk like ourselves and wanted to be our sales guy. He would load the boxes in his Mustang as soon as we made them, hit a few music stores and come back with a bunch of money. That's how we started the company.

From there we got enough money to have real relationships with real suppliers, and started developing more models. The main engineering people, Richard Neatrour and Tony Gambucurta, had been technicians at our audio repair shop. They went on to create the rest of MXR's product line, including the later digital stuff.

After a few years I sort of took off from the company. Rochester is a small town, and I didn't like being cooped up there. There were a lot of things that I wanted to do with my life. I moved back out to the West Coast. I was still working on stuff from there. I recall contributing to flanger designs, but I also wanted to pursue other things, such as chemistry. I would hang out with my friends at studios in L.A. and feel like I was learning a lot, but my absence from the company didn't do it any good.

Terry was the business guy—he would deal with the banks. He knew a little about engineering, but mainly he took care of MXR's financial business. We made some decisions that probably weren't the best. For example, we bought a big expensive building, and then interest rates hit the roof. Then Roland came in with a spectacular line of pedals. We were waving the American flag at MXR, but we had no idea how they could come up with a landed cost that was a tiny fraction of ours. Between that, the economy, and the business decisions we'd made, we really started to get tanked. At one point I just told everyone that I wanted to be off on my own. The other guys really liked hanging out with each other and didn't mind living in Rochester, so they scraped together the remains of MXR and founded Applied Research & Technology. I went off and

Two phasers, one choice.

MXR's circa-'83 Junior featured drum and percussion sounds.

made Alesis. A lot of things we started with at Alesis—such as the reverbs and drum machines —were things I'd developed at the tail end of MXR.

The remarkable part of this story is that we started from zero—less than zero, actually. Our hearts were definitely in it. For the 50 or so people involved, it was a magical part of our lives. We were doing something only older and better-financed people could do, and we were winning! The feeling of that is truly spectacular.

Richard Neatrour's Story

In 1972 I had just graduated from the Rochester Institute of Technology and was looking for work in the music business. While job hunting, I ran across Keith Barr and Terry Sherwood, who owned a stereo repair store in Rochester. I went to work for them that year doing warranty work on hi-fi gear.

The Loop Selector routed signals in different directions.

Originally Keith was interested in mixers, but after the Maestro phase shifters came out, we figured we could make similar products. Looking at the construction of most pedals and knowing where they broke down, we saw how we could improve on them.

Initially, our objective was to get the same audio performance with maybe a few different features, but make them rugged as hell. The die-cast boxes—and where we placed the knobs and jacks—were such that if they took a direct hit on concrete, they'd keep working. We also used op amps right from the beginning. At first we used 741s, then around '75 we started using Raytheon 4558s. Raytheon had a quality control problem, though, so we went to Dallas and talked Texas Instruments into making a 4558 for us. The Dynacomp was probably the first product to use an RCA 3080 VCA [voltage controlled amplifier]. We never made any handwired units. Even the first 50 or so boxes had printed circuit boards that we etched ourselves. After that we had them made by a PC board vendor.

The first four products we came out with—the Phase 90, Distortion Plus, Dynacomp, and the Blue Box—were all introduced within a couple of months of each other. Edgar Winter's octave-divided sound on "Frankenstein" inspired us to build the Blue Box. We sold a lot of those initially, but its use was somewhat limited and we eventually dropped it.

We made pedals in Keith and Terry's basement from September through December of '73. By January of '74 we'd gotten up to about 100 pieces per build, and there were more products that we wanted to make. We leased what became a fairly large manufacturing facility in an old part of town. Keith and I did most of the design work up until '76, when we started hiring other engineers. In the early days Keith concentrated more on the mechanical things. He was good at minimizing the number of parts needed for the quality we wanted.

MXR grew quickly, and we soon covered the range as far as what most other effects companies were offering. Looking around for something else guitarists might want, we came with couple of EQs, an envelope filter, and a number of other things that weren't available in pedal form. One of those was the Flanger, which was the first of its kind. Even before the Flanger, we came out with some modules designed to mount directly into mixing consoles. These were the Auto Flanger, Auto Phaser, and the Mini Limiter. You could mount up to eight of them in a rack.

Around '77 we decided to become more involved in studio effects. There wasn't a lot of competition—just EMT in Germany and Eventide here. That was a real learning experience. We got into digital logic, and from that point on, more than half of our products were digital. We came out with the Digital Delay, then the Flanger/Doubler and the Pitch Transposer.

In 1980 we moved into a facility that was probably a lot larger than we needed. We had a lot of overhead, and in hindsight we probably shouldn't have planned on that much growth. In the early '80s we were selling over 20,000 Distortion Plus pedals a year, but Boss and Ibanez were becoming more competitive, and our business began to dip. We came out with a lower-cost line of pedals called the Commande series that had plastic cases. They weren't very successful, though, so we introduced the 2000 series, which had die-cast metal cases. We continued to lose ground in the pedal market, but we were concentrating more on the rack stuff at that point anyway.

Too little, too late: The plastic-cased Commande series pedals were designed to boost sagging sales.

Terry and Keith wanted to take it easy after spending eight years getting the company to where it was. Between that and the increased competition from Japan, our profits decreased to the point where the bank wanted to close us down. It was a frustrating time for me because we had more product ideas and things we wanted to do. When the owners couldn't come to an agreement on a direction, a few of us got together and bought the rights to MXR. That's how we started Applied Research & Technology.

MU-TRON MUSICTRONICS

The '70s just wouldn't have been the same without Rosemont, New Jersey's Musitronics Corporation, producer of such innovative and roadworthy Mu-Tron pedals as the Phasor II, Bi-Phase, Octave Divider, Micro V envelope-controlled filter, Volume & Wah Pedal, and the Mu-Tron III, one of the most happening envelope-controlled filters ever created.

Musitronics also built the U.S. versions of Dan Armstrong's Orange Squeezer, Red Ranger, Purple Peaker, Yellow Humper, Blue Clipper, and Green Ringer. Musitronics founder Aaron Newman who left his job as chief engineer in Guild's electronics division to launch Mu-Tron in the summer of 1972 and product designer Mike Beigel provided their accounts of the Mu-Tron years.

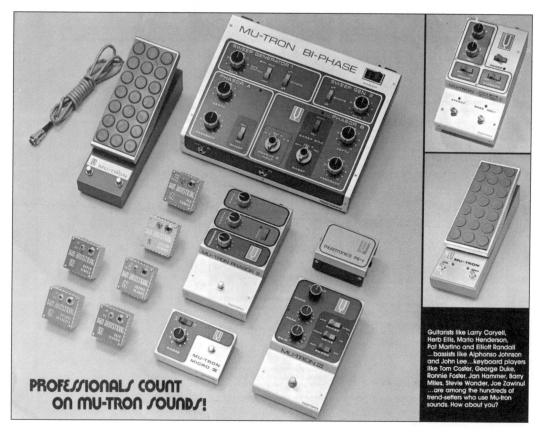

PROFESSIONALS COUNT ON MU-TRON SOUNDS!

Guitarists like Larry Coryell, Herb Ellis, Marlo Henderson, Pat Martino and Elliott Randall ...bassists like Alphonso Johnson and John Lee...keyboard players like Tom Coster, George Duke, Ronnie Foster, Jan Hammer, Barry Miles, Stevie Wonder, Joe Zawinul ...are among the hundreds of trend-setters who use Mu-Tron sounds. How about you?

Aaron Newman's Story

While I was at Guild we had a consultant named Mike Biegle. He and his partner Izzy Strauss had a company called Biegle-Strauss Labs, and they had developed a synthesizer that had an unusual controller. Al Dronge, who was Guild's president at that time, supported its development. Unfortunately, Al was killed in a plane crash, and the guy who replaced him wasn't interested in electronics. We had an amplifier plant in Elizabeth, New Jersey, and when Guild shut it down, I left the company. Mike Biegle and I discussed what kind of products we could make out of that synth technology. We wanted to make accessories rather than synthesizers. The first thing Mike came up with was the Mu-Tron III, an envelope follower and voltage-controlled filter.

Because of my years with Guild, I knew most of the major music dealers in the Northeast. I went around with a prototype of the Mu-Tron to stores such as Manny's in New York and Wurlitzer in Boston. The response was very enthusiastic, so we set about looking for some money. A music store owner in Farmington, New Jersey, named Derf Nolde provided a good deal of the start-up capital for the company that we now called Musitronics.

Musitronics began in a converted chicken coop in a very rural part of New Jersey, and remained there the entire time we were in business. Things really took off fast for us. Our first endorser was Larry Coryell, and our first major endorser was Stevie Wonder. We sent him a Mu-Tron III pedal and he fell in love with it. One day Stevie called to tell us he'd recorded a song called "Higher Ground" using a Hohner Clavinet through the Mu-Tron III.

113

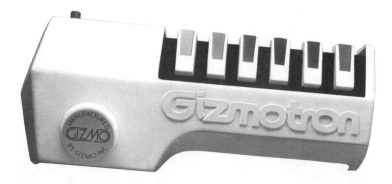

Our next product was the Phasor II and then the Bi-Phase, which was popular with keyboard players. Later we introduced the Octave Divider, which was designed by a friend of Dan Armstrong's named George Merriman. We also had an extremely good photo-electric volume/wah pedal, but that was near the end of our time and we never made very many.

The beginning of the end for us was around '77 when we got involved with a thing called the Gizmotron. It was an electromechanical bowing device brought to us by a sales rep who knew someone in the band 10cc. The Gizmotron was invented by band members Lol Creme and Kevin Godley, and they'd used it for the string-sounding parts on their hit "I'm Not in Love." The only problem was that Lol was the only person who could actually play the thing. We were blown away by the Gizmo's potential, but in hindsight, we should have realized that it couldn't work. The Gizmo had some physical limitations that you couldn't really overcome. For instance, we discovered that if we made them during

the winter, they wouldn't work properly in hot weather. It was the characteristics of the plastics, and none of us were plastics engineers. We were out of our realm.

Musitronics didn't have enough money to keep going with both the Gizmotron and the Mu-Tron line, so the company directors decided to sell Musitronics. Unfortunately, that's when we found ARP, a synthesizer company that was in the process of committing suicide with a guitar synth called the Avatar. We sold Musitronics to them in '78 on a royalty basis, but they folded before we could ever collect a cent. We became Gizmo Incorporated and continued to try to make it go, but then I had a heart attack and that was the end of it.

The Mu-Tron thing was tremendous fun. It was a challenge because we never had enough money. Not that Mu-Tron lost a lot of money, but we just sort of plodded along. We had lots of big-name musicians using our products, but our phaser cost a hell of a lot more to make than the MXR or Electro-Harmonix phasers. We were determined to build the best products that we could. I think if we had been more efficient, we might have lowered our costs enough to survive.

Mike Beigel's Story

My electronic-music experimentation began in 1967 when I started playing my clarinet into the soundhole of an acoustic-electric 12-string with the volume turned all the way up. At the time I was trying to obtain a simulated drone-string accompaniment to clarinet improvisation. In '68 I proposed an electronics project titled "Source Dependent Musical Instrument" for one of my courses at MIT, and this turned into the thesis for my degrees.

I got an engineering degree and a humanities degree—I was MIT's first electronic music graduate—and between '68 and '69 I built a strange analog device that simulated a drone-string accompaniment to an arbitrary musical sound input. The system diagram was basically a blueprint for every kind of instrument-controlled effect and synthesizer made. Around this time a friend of mine named Izzy Strauss and I also developed a real synthesizer that used very different musical controllers. Guild Musical Instruments bought into the project in '70, and we began making synthesizer prototypes for them.

These synths were different because they had very strange hand controllers. I could play music on them, but they looked and acted like nothing made before or since. They never went into production, however, because Guild's president died in an airplane crash and the rest of the company wasn't interested in electronic music.

In '72 Aaron Newman and I decided to extract some sections from the synthesizer and see if we could make a new product out of it. First we hooked up an opto-elec-

tronic-based envelope-controlled filter, tweaked it and turned it into a little product. Digital audio pioneer [and former AES president] Barry Blesser also participated in its design. We first called it the Auto Wah and then marketed it as the Mu-Tron III. Synthesizer inventor Bob Moog's affidavit helped us get the patent. The Mu-Tron III became quite popular thanks in part to Stevie Wonder, who helped immensely by giving us free publicity and letting us use his name.

In '73 we prototyped a bucket-brigade flanger, but then immediately shelved it for a phase shifter. At the time phase shifters were more popular and a whole lot easier to make. The Mu-Tron Phasor used transconductance op-amps for the variable element at a time when most people were using FETs.

We were aware of most of the effects that were around, but the phase shifter that we were going after was Maestro's PS-1. MXR also came out with the Phase 90 while we were designing the Phasor, but we gave ours two more stages. Then in '74 came the Mu-Tron Bi-Phase, which was actually Newman's idea. We made it with photo mods because we wanted a really wide dynamic range. Though the technology was semi-obsolete—even at that time—the photo mod helped give the Phasor its own sound because photo resistors don't track each other

exactly and each has its own particular time constant and subtle form of non-linearity. We even had a special photo mod custom made for us with six photocells in it.

At first the Bi-Phase prototypes sounded too clean, and we didn't know what to do about it. All the FET-based phasers had a non-linearity to them. In audio terms ours was too good, but in musical terms it wasn't good enough. I decided to put a feedback control around the phase-shift loop so that instead of distorting the signal it emphasized the peaks where the phase shifter didn't cancel the signal. This made the sound more interesting without distorting it. Our Bi-Phase was the first phaser with a feedback pot, though Electro-Harmonix got a phase shifter to market before us with a feedback switch.

I made sure the Bi-Phase had as many ways of being controlled with oscillators, pedals or external inputs that I could possibly stick into one box. When we designed the Opti-Pot C-100 control pedal for the Bi-Phase, we wanted to make something that was way high tech compared with everything else. One was the mechanism itself—which was spring-loaded and connected with a Delrin hinge—and the other was its opto-electronic linearized control, which basically replaced the pot with a photo-transistor.

Mu-Tron III and George Merriman-designed Octave Divider.

After the Bi-Phase we made the Phaser II, which was one-half of a Bi-Phase with only an oscillator sweep control. That was probably our most-popular product. For the Mu-Tron Octave Divider, we joined with Dan Armstrong and George Merriman. We started producing Armstrong's line of products, and we got Merriman working with us on the Octave Divider. The last products we introduced were the Vol-Wah pedal and the Flanger. The pedal- and LFO-controlled Flanger was quite a piece of work, but that was right before we sold Musitronics to the ARP Instrument Company. We only made about a thousand of them.

The Gizmotron was the great disaster. I had wanted to go into digital audio at the time. I liked the Gizmotron a lot when I first heard it, but it basically ate the company because there wasn't enough money to do R&D on the Gizmontron and digital audio at the same time. Against my strenuous objections the board of directors decided to sell Musitronics.

In '80 I introduced the Beigel Sound Lab Envelope Controlled Filter—of which only 50 were produced— and also developed the Resynator Instrument Controlled Synthesizer for a company called Musico. I also designed a mixer for St. Louis

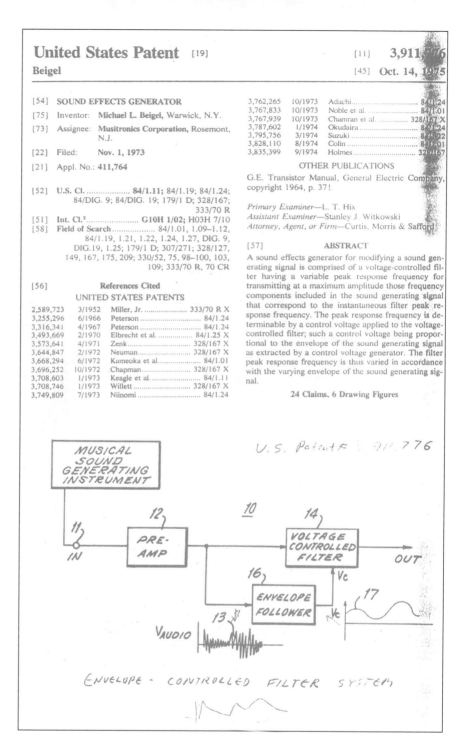

United States Patent [19]

Beigel

[11] 3,911,776

[45] Oct. 14, 1975

[54] **SOUND EFFECTS GENERATOR**

[75] Inventor: **Michael L. Beigel**, Warwick, N.Y.

[73] Assignee: **Musitronics Corporation**, Rosemont, N.J.

[22] Filed: **Nov. 1, 1973**

[21] Appl. No.: **411,764**

[52] U.S. Cl. 84/1.11; 84/1.19; 84/1.24;
84/DIG. 9; 84/DIG. 19; 179/1 D; 328/167;
333/70 R

[51] Int. Cl.² G10H 1/02; H03H 7/10

[58] Field of Search 84/1.01, 1.09–1.12,
84/1.19, 1.21, 1.22, 1.24, 1.27, DIG. 9,
DIG.19, 1.25; 179/1 D; 307/271; 328/127,
149, 167, 175, 209; 330/52, 75, 98–100, 103,
109; 333/70 R, 70 CR

[56] **References Cited**

UNITED STATES PATENTS

2,589,723	3/1952	Miller, Jr.	333/70 R X
3,255,296	6/1966	Peterson	84/1.24
3,316,341	4/1967	Peterson	84/1.24
3,493,669	2/1970	Elbrecht et al.	84/1.25 X
3,573,641	4/1971	Zenk	328/167 X
3,644,847	2/1972	Neuman	328/167 X
3,668,294	6/1972	Kumeoka et al.	84/1.01
3,696,252	10/1972	Chapman	328/167 X
3,708,603	1/1973	Keagle et al.	84/1.11
3,708,746	1/1973	Willett	328/167 X
3,749,809	7/1973	Niinomi	84/1.24
3,762,265	10/1973	Adachi	84/1.24
3,767,833	10/1973	Noble et al.	84/1.01
3,767,939	10/1973	Chamran et al.	328/167 X
3,787,602	1/1974	Okudaira	84/1.24
3,795,756	3/1974	Suzuki	84/1.22
3,828,110	8/1974	Colin	84/1.01
3,835,399	9/1974	Holmes	328/167

OTHER PUBLICATIONS

G.E. Transistor Manual, General Electric Company, copyright 1964, p. 371.

Primary Examiner—L. T. Hix
Assistant Examiner—Stanley J. Witkowski
Attorney, Agent, or Firm—Curtis, Morris & Safford

[57] **ABSTRACT**

A sound effects generator for modifying a sound generating signal is comprised of a voltage-controlled filter having a variable peak response frequency for transmitting at a maximum amplitude those frequency components included in the sound generating signal that correspond to the instantaneous filter peak response frequency. The peak response frequency is determinable by a control voltage applied to the voltage-controlled filter; such a control voltage being proportional to the envelope of the sound generating signal as extracted by a control voltage generator. The filter peak response frequency is thus varied in accordance with the varying envelope of the sound generating signal.

24 Claims, 6 Drawing Figures

Music. From '79 to '96 I was heavily involved in the development of RFID products [radio frequency identification, now a global industry with applications in many fields of identification, security and scientific research], which allowed animals to be tagged with a miniature transmitter implanted under their skin. Through my involvement with RFID, I learned about new technologies including ultra-miniaturization, surface-mount design, digital-analog techniques and advanced manufacturing methods.

236,212

ELECTRONIC MUSICAL ACCESSORY

Michael L. Beigel, Warwick, Herbert Ross, Bronx, and Alan R. Wallerstein, Freeport, N.Y., assignors to Musitronics Corporation, Rosemont, N.J.

Filed May 17, 1973, Ser. No. 361,273

Term of patent 14 years

Int. Cl. D14—99

U.S. Cl. D26—14 L

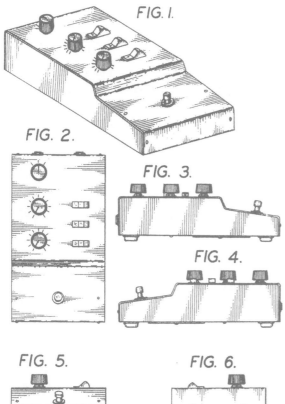

FIG. 1 is a perspective view of our design for an electronic musical accessory;
FIG. 2 is a top plan view thereof;
FIG. 3 is a left side elevational view thereof;
FIG. 4 is a right side elevational view thereof;
FIG. 5 is a front end view thereof; and
FIG. 6 is a rear end view thereof.
We claim:
The ornamental design for an electronic musical accessory, as shown.

References Cited

UNITED STATES PATENTS

D. 210,026   1/1968   Kahn _____ D26—14 M

OTHER REFERENCES

Grossman Music Corp., Cat. 68, © 1968, p. 467, Kent 6400 Distorter.
Lafayette Electronics, © 1972, p. 180, Super Fuzz, sound effects generator.

BERNARD ANSHER, Primary Examiner

In '94 I met former competitor Mike Matthews [president of Sovtek/Electro-Harmonix] at a NAMM show. We talked about effects pedals, and later he asked me if I'd be interested in re-creating the Mu-Tron III for Electro-Harmonix. The new box, which is called the Q-Tron, uses the same opto-electronic design of the Mu-Tron III, but I've given it some new features and improved its specs. It will be followed by other new types of effects devices. It's great to be involved again in the musical products industry after quite an extended "vacation."

PRO CO

One of the most popular late-'70s distorters was the Pro Co Rat, a state-of-the-art stomper that offered an amazingly wide tonal range courtesy of its uniquely voiced filter control. The Kalamazoo, Michigan, company—which also produces instrument and microphone cables, direct boxes, patching systems, and other pro sound products—traces its roots to the mid '60s and the repair/P.A. department of Kalamazoo's Rock & Drum Shack, a subsidiary of the long-defunct Dodds-Davidson music chain. Charlie Wicks—the Shack's P.A.-department manager and now president of Pro Co—bought out the Rock & Drum Shack in '70 and started the Sound Factory (Pro Co's predecessor) at 135 East Kalamazoo Avenue. Pro Co has operated from this location ever since.

The sheet-metal-enclosed Rat debuted in '79 and was followed by a more-compact model in '84. In '87 came the Rat 2 with its glow-in-the-dark graphics and triangular LED bypass indicator, and the R2DU "Dual Rack Rat," which offered two identical Rat circuits in a one-rack-space unit. Remote switching for the R2DU was via the RFS-2 dual footswitch. The Turbo Rat appeared in '89 sporting a sloped-front housing, glowing graphics, and a 2.8-volt output—more than double that of its litter mates. Pro Co also produced a bass fuzz called the Juggernaut, which was available from '79 to '84.

Three generations:
The Rat, Rat 2 and Turbo Rat.

Pro Co senior engineer Steve Kiraly and ex-Pro Co engineering director and Rat designer Scott Burnham (now an audio technician for Creative Ink) provided a history of the Rat's development.

Steve Kiraly's Story

Back in the Doors and Jimi Hendrix days, the fuzz of choice was the Dallas-Arbiter Fuzz Face. Lots of guitar players, both famous and unknown, would bring their Fuzz Faces to us, and I would tweak them for more gain. I wasn't into reinventing the wheel, so I simply removed the original British low-gain transistors and replaced them with substantially higher-gain RCA transistors. That was my sleazy way of hot-rodding the old Fuzz Face.

Our ex-director of engineering, Scott Richard Burnham, was 110 percent fanatic. He thought my cheesy method of trading out the transistors was way too easy, so he designed a whole new distortion device from the ground up, using an integrated circuit and an FET follower. What he was trying to do was technically far and beyond what anybody in the distortion-device business was doing back in '76.

Originally the Rat was intended to be a custom-made pedal—we never thought about mass-producing it. We took the orders first and then we built them. At first we made small batches of a dozen or so in little Hammond project boxes, and all the holes were hand-drilled. Very early ones had a black crinkle finish, and a friend of ours would silk-screen the name in bright fluorescent letters with a graphic image of a rat. The first dozen were made that way.

Around 1979 we started manufacturing the Rat in large numbers. For the first production units we went to a local sheet-metal fabrication house. That's when Scott

Two rats in one nest: The rackmountable R2DU and footswitch.

designed the heavy-duty wrap-around 20-gauge enclosure. We still make a Vintage Rat that closely approximates the construction of those early ones. Then we went to a clamshell-type enclosure, which had a 12-gauge U-shaped base that held the PC board. They were solid black with white lettering. In the late '80s we introduced the Rat 2 and then the Turbo Rat, which had a sloped front and Lexan/Mylar glow-in-the-dark graphics.

The early Rats used tantalum capacitors. The first tonal change happened when we switched to Mylar caps, and the second when we added the LED. The earliest Rats had true input-output switching. We used a nice 15-amp mechanical switch that switched both the input side and the output side, so straight through was like a piece of wire. When we put in the LED, one pole of the two-pole double-throw switch had to be common to

PRO-CO SOUND PRESENTS *THE RAT*

GUARANTEED TO DISTORT LIKE HELL

[Total Harmonic Distortion (T.H.D.) = 39%]

THE SWEET SOUND

Designed for smooth, "fat" distortion and effortless sustain even at minimal volume levels, the Rat offers the guitar player a richly raunchy lead sound at the punch of a footswitch. The distortion intensity, tonality and output level are all continuously variable to suit the individual player's needs and tastes. The sound is warm and thick, far superior to any previously available commercial distortion device. It is also startlingly effective on bass guitar, electric piano, synthesizers and clavinet.

BUT SOUND IS ONLY HALF THE STORY

The construction of the Rat is of the same high quality as any Pro-Co Sound product. Carbon film resistors are used for low noise, tantalum capacitors for low leakage, special op-amps for low current drain. A tough Carling footswitch and the smooth conductive plastic elements of the Clarostat controls insure long and reliable life. Assembled on a mil-spec G-10 epoxy-glass circuit board and housed in its rugged, 20-gauge welded steel chassis, the Rat is built to survive years of demanding service, whether in clubs, concert halls, or the recording studio.

SPECIFICATIONS

Input Impedance	Greater than 500K ohms for minimal loading effect on instrument.
Output Impedance	Approximately 1K ohms source.
Recommended Output Load	Greater than 10K ohms.
Maximum Output Level	1 volt p-p, virtual square wave.
Tone Control	Variable 6 dB/octave low-pass filter.
T.H.D.	39%
Power Requirements	9V battery (Mallory MN 1604 recommended) or 9V. D.C. adapter via 1/8″ miniature phone jack.
Current Drain	Less than 2 mA at 9V. D.C..
Dimensions	3-1/8″H. × 5″ W. × 4-1/2″ D.
Weight	1-1/2 lbs.

UNPLUG THE INPUT CABLE TO SHUT OFF THE BATTERY WHEN NOT IN USE.

KALAMAZOO, MICHIGAN 49007

---

the output circuit to give us a return path to turn the LED on and off. It caused enough tonal difference that we reintroduced the Vintage Rat in the sheet-metal box, which has no LED and no external loading from the electronics.

About 20 years after the Rat was designed, somebody asked if we could put two of them in a rack unit. So we cobbled one together using the same PC boards that were in the regular production rack. We mounted the boards in a single space Hammond or Middle Atlantic rack box, added control relays for turning it on and off, LEDs to show which Rat was on, and enough power-supply bypassing so the units didn't interact with each other.

Then the R2DU orders started coming in. By now, though, we were starting to learn. After hand-building five or six more of them, we decided to draw it up with a single PC board that had the circuitry of two Rats, a place to locate the relays and all the power-supply stuff. It was sort of designed to be automatically assembled, even though—as in the case with all of our effects—they were never designed for manufacturability. We just never thought we'd have to make a whole bunch of them.

Scott Burnham's Story

I began working formally for Pro Co in '75, but I had worked for the Sound Factory in '72 and '73. During those years I listened mostly to progressive stuff. To my ear, Steve Howe from Yes was the best. He was so versatile and he had such a palette of colors. Another player who influenced me in the development of the Rat was John McLaughlin. He was playing a Les Paul, and he had the most crazed and unbelievably overdriven sound. Those were the kinds of tones that impressed me, and I was trying to figure out how I could make my Strat sound similar.

Classic sheetmetal.

At this time there was a company in Kalamazoo called Systems & Technology In Music, which was owned by an ex-Moog rep named Greg Hockman. One of their designers was another Moog vet named Ritchie Walborn, who had done a world tour with Emerson, Lake & Palmer. During that tour, Greg Lake had picked up four Fender Concerts that he wanted to use simultaneously. Since you couldn't hang four amps across the output of a Les Paul without loading it down excessively, Ritchie whipped up this little switchable pre-amp that had about 18dB of boost, and he put it in Greg's guitar.

When Systems & Technology came about, they decided to make a product based on that circuit called the Overdrive. The original Overdrive was not a fuzztone. It was basically a bandpass filter, so it was like a wah-wah pedal that was always switched on. You could boost bass, mids, and highs, but it always had a certain resonance to it. The Overdrive was murderous. I've seen people plug it in thinking it was a fuzzbox, and practically get their heads blown off.

Since that was kind of a problem, Systems designed another Overdrive that actually was a fuzz. That

124

second version introduced two ideas that I later lifted: using a couple of diodes for clipping and having an FET input buffer that was always on. That was a hip thing to me because they were worried about the signal loading that occurs when you hook two pedals in series. That FET circuit existed in the original dozen Rats, but was later dropped in favor of a true straight-wire bypass.

Ritchie later came up with a mod for the original Overdrive that added an FET at the output and a pot to control the volume. I did a few of those mods for people, and everyone seemed to think it sounded better than the new Overdrive fuzz. The original Overdrive later became known as the Harmonic Energizer—Frank Zappa was a fan of those.

I was dabbling in modifying Systems & Technology pedals, trying to come up with something of my own because I didn't really like anything that was out there. I liked bits and pieces of different things. The idea for the Rat was to have an input buffer first, then an op-amp to crank it way up. The signal would then be rammed across a couple of parallel diodes that clipped the hell out of it, then sent it through a FET to smooth things out.

Juggernaut bass fuzz.

I had the basic circuit roughed together and I'd found an op-amp I liked, the LM 308N, which was an instrumentation amp used for seismic and medical sensors. I was experimenting with an EQ boost for this op-amp in order to pre-boost the treble so I could use just a passive tone control to cut back the highs. I was bypassing the voltage divider that sets the gain when I picked up a resistor, looked at it and thought to myself, "Yellow, violet, brown—that's 470Ω." I plugged it in, expecting to get about 50dB of gain, but when I picked up my Strat and hit a string, it went wooooo. I thought, "Holy shit, this is cool. What did I do?"

I looked real closely and realized that I'd plugged in a 47Ω resistor instead of a 470Ω resistor. That meant it had somewhere around 70dB of gain, which, according to its spec sheet, was impossible from that op-amp. Trying to set the gain on this thing, I had stumbled across a combination of resistors that produced this really weird

One of the first 12.

high-frequency shelving boost that the op-amp couldn't possibly sustain. It didn't have enough slew rate to produce that much gain at those frequencies, so it drove the op-amp into incredible slewing distortion. This usually is very bad, but in this case it's what gave the Rat its weird sort of yeowl—I've never heard any other stompbox make that sound.

Just to make sure it wasn't a fluke, I stripped the circuit off the proto board and rebuilt it completely using different parts with the same values. After it happened again, I realized that this was actually going to work. The whole thing was caused by plugging the wrong resistor into the proto board. If I'd read the resistor color bands correctly the first time, the Rat probably never would have happened.

People make a big deal about the Rat's filter control, but it's just a simple-stupid high-frequency roll-off that uses a variable resistor in series with a shunt capacitor. On the first Rats it was called a tone control. Later I real-

ized that if I hooked it up the opposite way using a log-taper pot, it reduced highs as you turned it up and increased highs as you turned it down. That's when I started calling it a filter control.

Around the time we put out the Turbo Rat—which was simply a Rat with different diodes—I built a prototype Rat that used germanium transistors. They clip at half the input of a silicon diode and give even more sustain and compression. A germanium transistor breaks down at .3 volts instead of .7 volts, and the result is that everything clips a bit sooner. I even suggested that we build a Rat with a dip switch on the bottom so the player could select between silicon, germanium, or gallium-arsenide transistors. But my time was being monopolized doing custom turnkey cabling setups for recording studios and commercial sound companies.

We originally made 12 crinkle-finish Rats. One has no silk-screened graphics, and that's the prototype. Those have the FET input buffer and the tone control, and they used a square Bud CU442 steel box. In early '78

we built 100 production units, each with a single-pole bypass switch. After they were all made, I listened to one real closely in bypass mode, and I could hear the distortion bleeding through to the output. I remember having to take all the single-pole switches out of those units and replace them with double-pole switches. That's why the circuit boards don't match the switches on those first Rats.

During the first few years of production, Rats were made mostly by a guy named Randy Piotroski. Right from the start we used PC boards, and I chose tantalum caps because I thought they were cool and because NASA used them. At that stage I wasn't interested in pinching pennies. If each Rat cost 25 cents more to build and we made 100, that was only 25 bucks—big deal. When we started making over 20,000 per year, we switched to tubular-aluminum electrolytic caps. It didn't seem to make any sonic difference at the time, but later some players told me that the tantalum-equipped Rats sounded different than the new ones. Just to be sure, we built a few more Rats with tantalum caps and compared them with our current production models. We couldn't hear a difference. The only thing we could surmise was that there was a difference in the way those original tantalum caps had aged.

My favorite Rat is the one I call the Jeff Beck model. It has the heavy-duty enclosure with the 12-gauge U-shaped base, but it doesn't have the LED. It's the original blunt instrument—I like the way it feels when I pick one up. Nile Rodgers used one when he was in Sheik, and I think he then turned Beck onto it during the Flash sessions. There are some pictures of Jeff in the Power Station studio with a Rat sitting on an amp next to him. When I heard Beck's solo on "People Get Ready," it gave me the chills. I said, "That's my sound. That's my fuzztone."

ROLAND / BOSS

Roland was founded in 1972 by electronics engineer Ikataro Kakahashi, inventor of the programmable drum machine and one-time employee of Hammond Organ in Japan. Kakahashi's first solo venture was a drum-machine company called Ace Tone; legend has it he changed the name to Roland because he was afraid people would call the company "Acid Tone." Roland initially made synthesizers, drum machines, and guitar amps. Ace Tone's technology led directly to Roland's popular TR series programmable drum machines.

Roland's venture into effects began with the RE-101, RE-201, RE-301, and RE-501 Space Echoes. All but the RE-101 featured either reverb or reverb plus chorus along with tape echo. Another Roland first was chorusing, a stupendously popular effect that was offered in some stand-alone devices such as the DC-50 and DC-30 analog chorus/echo. Other early stand-alones were the DC-10 analog echo and the RV-100 analog reverb.

Roland also made a number of pre-Boss pedals, including the AF-100 Bee Baa and AF-60 Bee Gee fuzztones, AS-1 Sustainer, AG-5 Funny Cat (auto wah plus distortion), AD-50 Double Beat (fuzz and wah), AW-10 Wah Beat (wah-wah), AP-7 Jet Phaser, and AP-2 Phase Two. All sported heavy cast-metal enclosures, except for the stainless-steel Bee Baa and Funny Cat.

ROLAND EFFECTORS

The easy way to mellow sounds.

AP-7 JET PHASER

The JET PHASER/AP-7 is a phase shifter producing dynamic jet sounds for rock guitars.

● Changeover Switches: Effect/Normal, Fast/Slow ● Controls: Jet level, Mode Selector (Jet 1,2,3,4/Phase 1,2), Resonance, Slow rate ● Batteries (006P : 9V) ● Dimensions: 252 (W) x 170 (H) x 70 (D) mm (9.92'' x 6.65'' x 2.75'') ● Weight: 1600g (3.52lbs.)

AP-2 PHASE TWO

PHASE II/AP-2 is a compact phase shifter with simplified controls, including a "Resonance" control for enhancing the phase effect.

● Effect/Normal Changeover Switch ● Controls: Rate, Resonance ● Batteries (006P : 9V) ● Dimensions: 62 (W) x 115 (H) x 205 (D) mm (2.44'' x 4.52'' x 80.7'') ● Weight: 850g (1.87lbs.)

Expands the total effect.

AF-100 BEE BAA

The AF-100 is Roland's number one fuzz unit, providing a wide range of fuzz control.

● Changeover Switches: Effect / Normal, Fuzz & Treble booster, Fuzz tone ● Knobs: Fuzz sustain, Fuzz tone, Fuzz volume, Treble booster volume ● Battery: 006P (9V) ● Dimensions: 230 x 165 x 65 mm (9.1'' x 6.5'' x 2.6'') ● Weight: 1050g (2.31lbs.)

AF-60 BEE GEE

The AF-60 is a compactly designed fuzz unit with "Tone" and "Out level" controls and a Fuzz/Normal changeover switch.

● Changeover Switch: Fuzz / Normal ● Control Knobs: Tone, Out level ● Battery: 006P (9V) ● Dimensions: 62 x 115 x 205 mm (2.5'' x 4.5'' x 8.1'') ● Weight: 850g (1.87lbs.)

AS-1 SUSTAINER

The AS-1 is a unique sustainer which sustains the original sound without distortion, unlike fuzz effect distortion sustainers.

● Changeover Switch: Sustain / Normal ● Control Knobs: Sustain, Out level ● Batteries: 006P (9V) ● Dimensions: 62 x 115 x 205 mm (2.5'' x 4.5'' x 8.1'') ● Weight: 850g (1.87lbs.)

AG-5 FUNNY CAT

The AG-5 provides both auto-wah and soft distortion effects simultaneously or separately.

● Changeover Switches: SDS / Normal, Harmonic mover / Normal ● Control Knobs: SDS level, Harmonic mover effect, Harmonic mover made changeover switch (3 steps: A,B, and C) ● Battery: 006P (9V) ● Dimensions: 230 x 165 x 65 mm (9.1'' x 6.5'' x 2.6'') ● Weight: 1050g (2.31lbs.)

AD-50 DOUBLE BEAT

The AD-50 combines fuzz and wah effects and wah effects.

● Changeover Switches: Wah / Normal, Fuzz / Normal ● Control Knobs: Fuzz sustain, Fuzz out level, Fuzz tone selector ● Battery: 006P (9V) ● Dimensions: 80 x 160 x 275 mm (3.2'' x 6.3'' x 10.8'') ● Weight: 1850g (4.07 lbs.)

AW-10 WAH BEAT

The AW-10 is a highly dependable wah-pedal providing sharp sound change.

● Changeover Switch: Wah / Normal ● Battery: 006P (9V) ● Dimensions: 80 x 110 x 275 mm (3.2'' x 4.3'' x 10.8'') ● Weight 1380g (3.04lbs.)

Roland's late-'70s lineup.

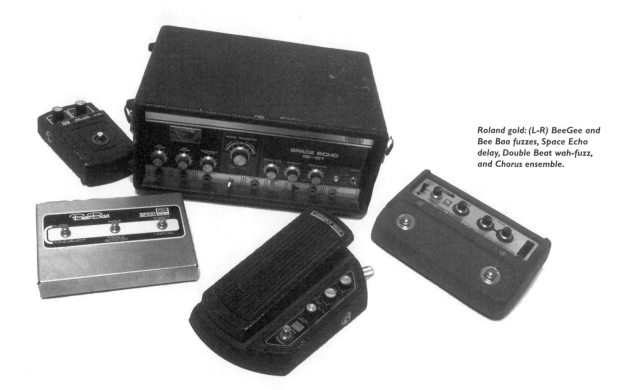

Roland gold: (L-R) BeeGee and Bee Baa fuzzes, Space Echo delay, Double Beat wah-fuzz, and Chorus ensemble.

In the early '80s Roland's effects line expanded to include the SDE series digital delays and other rackmount devices. Stevie Ray Vaughan used a Roland SDD-320 Dimension D for his solos on David Bowie's *Let's Dance*. "It seems to work a little like a stereo chorus," Stevie said in a 1983 *Guitar Player* interview. "You take a note that was hit hard, and it makes it sound more ornery and a little fatter." Nonetheless, Roland's ads for the device sounded almost apologetic: "It won't blow you away—it isn't supposed to. That's because some effects are not measured by their intensity, but by their subtlety."

Roland's Boss division was launched by Roland USA's Tom Beckman, who served as company president from 1972 to 1993. The first Boss product was an acoustic guitar pickup and preamp called The Boss. It was followed in 1976 by a series of cast-metal-cased pedals (similar to Roland's) that included the CE-1 Chorus Ensemble, DB-5 Driver (distortion plus 5-band graphic EQ), DM-1 Delay Machine, and BF-1 Flanger. The company's now-familiar stompbox line debuted that same year with the CS-1 Compression Sustainer, PH-1 Phaser, OD-1 Overdrive, SP-1 Spectrum (parametric filter), DS-1 Distortion, NF-1 Noise Gate, SG-1 Slow Gear, TW-1 Touch Wah, GE-6 graphic EQ, and CE-2 chorus. A pair of rocker-style pedals—the PW-1 Rocker Wah and PD-1 Rocker Distortion—were also offered.

The stompbox-sized Mascot amplifier.

According to Boss marketing manager Paul Youngblood, "We wanted to make real tough effects that you could stomp on, drive over, or pour beer into. Before leaving the factory, each pedal is plugged in and smashed around by hand to make sure all the components are solid. Three people hand-test every single pedal this way.

"We've never changed our design. The very first pedals look just like the ones we make now. Even the color coordination remains the same. The blue pedals are chorus, black is metal distortion, the overdrives are orange, power supplies are red, the delays are silver, and compressors are dark blue. Our line always consists of around 30 devices. We discontinue certain models if a better one comes out, but some hang around forever. The DS-1 distortion unit has been a mainstay since Day One, and we still sell it.

"One unique thing about this company is that the engineers are not only extremely capable designers, but outstanding guitarists as well. Every one of them is a monster."

A Pocket Full of Boss

Volume 1 of *The Boss Pocket Dictionary* lists these effects and accessories: NF-1 Noise Gate, CS-2 Compression Sustainer, GE-7 Equalizer, DS-1 Distortion, OD-1 Overdrive, SD-1 Super Overdrive, HM-2 Heavy Metal, PH-1R Phaser, BF-2 Flanger, TW-1 T Wah, OC-2 Octave, VB-2 Vibrato, CE-3 Chorus, DM-3 Delay, DD-2 Digital Delay, DE-200 Digital Delay, RX-100 Reverb Box, PW-1 Rocker Wah, PV-1 Rocker Volume, FV-200 Keyboard Volume, FV-100 Guitar Volume, HC-2 Hand Clapper, PC-2 Percussion Synthesizer, BCB-6 Carrying Box (a molded plastic case that doubled as a pedalboard), DB-33 Dr. Beat, DR-110 Dr. Rhythm, and the GE-10 Graphic Equalizer.

RE-301 ECHO CHAMBER

The professional echo with sound-on-sound, chorus, and reverb.

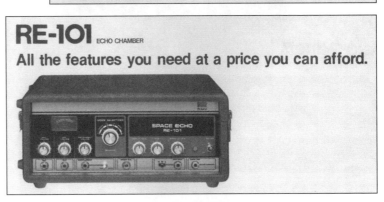

RE-101 ECHO CHAMBER

All the features you need at a price you can afford.

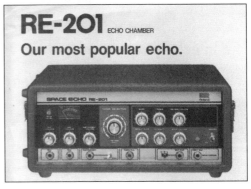

RE-201 ECHO CHAMBER

Our most popular echo.

131

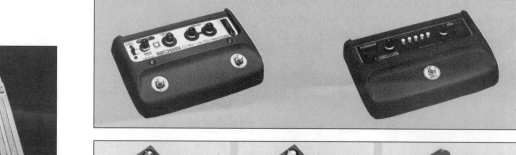

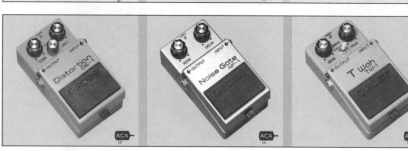

The *Pocket Dictionary* also featured several pedal configurations designed to replicate the guitar sounds from popular songs, including Journey's "Separate Ways," the Police's "Every Breath You Take," Pat Metheny's "Heartland," and "Maniac" from Michael Sembello's Flashback soundtrack.

Volume 2 of the *Pocket Dictionary* adds the DSD-2 Digital Sampler/Delay and PH-2 Super Phaser, as well as the Micro Studio Series, a line of half-rack-space effects aimed at the burgeoning home-recording market: the RDD-10 Digital Delay, RBF-10 Flanger, RPH-10 Phaser, RCL-10 Compressor/Limiter, RGE-10 Graphic Equalizer, DE-200 Digital Delay, and CE-300 Super Chorus. In 1987 Boss expanded the line with the RDD-20 Digital Delay, RCE-10 Digital Chorus Ensemble, RPQ-1-Preamp/ Parametric EQ, RPS-10 Digital Pitch Shifter/Delay, and ROD-10 Overdrive/ Distortion.

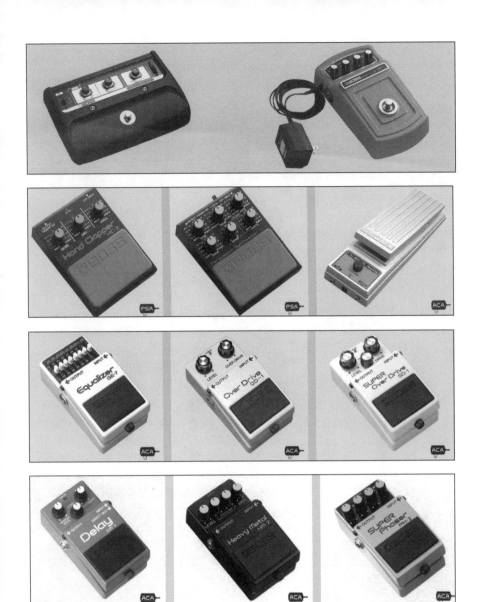

By 1989 Boss had upped its stompbox offerings to 27 with the addition of the OD-2 Turbo Overdrive, DS-2 Turbo Distortion, DF-2 Super Feedbacker & Distortion, MZ-2 Digital Metalizer, DD-3 Digital Delay, DSD-3 Digital Sampler/Delay, RV-2 Digital Reverb, PS-2 Digital Pitch Shifter/Delay, CE-2 Chorus, DC-3 Digital Dimension, HF-2 High Band Flanger, NS-2 Noise Suppressor, FT-2 Dynamic Filter, GE-7B Bass Equalizer, CE-2B Bass Chorus, and BF-2B Bass Flanger. The RPD-10 Digital Panning Delay joined the Micro Studio Series.

The Heavy Metal's '87 debut.

133

SEAMOON

The pedal scene is littered with the transistorized husks of long-goners such as Seamoon, a small and short-lived company founded in the early '70s by John Lang, owner of Skatzenbags Music in Berkeley, California. Lang was a stompbox entrepreneur who contracted with local electronics techs for his circuit designs, which he then built and marketed.

Seamoon's offerings included the Fresh Fuzz and Final Phase (both Lee Powell designs), the Studio Flanger (designed by David Tarnowsky, who later formed ADA), the Funk Machine envelope follower (a Craig Anderton design), and a couple of solid-state combo amps. The earliest Seamoon effects used plastic casings. Later units had folded-sheet-metal enclosures, then cast-aluminum boxes that may have inspired ADA's.

After Seamoon's demise, Lang started an even shorter-lived company called JXL. The Flanger and the Final Phase were JXL's only products, and the whole affair lasted only a few months. When JXL was laid to rest, Tarnowsky reclaimed those designs and reissued them as ADA products. "I kept Lee's basic concept in the Final Phase of adding distortion ahead of the phase-shifting circuit," Tarnowsky says, "but I completely redesigned the phase shifter."

Rap sheet for Seamoon's Studio Flanger and Funk Machine.

The Seamoon Ltd. **STUDIO FLANGER** is an exciting new experience in "analog delay" flanging and sound modification. The variable delay encountered in the **STUDIO FLANGER** makes a myriad of sounds available, including, Flanging, Intensified Phase Shifting, (43,200°) phase shift. 120 notches at 15Khz), Vibrato, Spectrum Shifting, Harmonic Shifting, Intensified Leslie, as well as many other Recording Studio sounds. Electronically the **STUDIO FLANGER** is equal to about 50 phase shifters working in unison, which makes an infinate number of sounds possible.

For quiet operation the **STUDIO FLANGER** is equiped with a "noise gate" which will eliminate all extraneous noise while the unit is on but no signal is being played through it. All electronic musical devices including sound reinforcement systems will be enhanced by the **STUDIO FLANGER**. Its versatility along with its simplicity in use is why it is the musicians choice.

Additionally the unit is equiped with a battery eliminator with a non-shorting type jack & plug which precludes the need for batteries.

The electronics are encased in a strong cast aluminum case, trimmed with a silvered face plate, accented by multi-colored graphics. The footswitch is an in/out switch which bypasses the electronics when the unit is not in use.

The Seamoon Ltd. **FUNK MACHINE** has become a standard with more than 70 national and international recording artists. Its familiar sound can be heard on records in all types of music from Funk, to Jazz, to Rock, to Country. The effect is similar to that of a Wa Wa with the notable exception that it is completely controlled by the emphasis of the players attack. The harder the attack, the more intense is the **FUNK EFFECT.**

The **FUNK MACHINE** is designed to be used with Electric Guitar, Fender Rhodes Piano, Clavinet, and horns, but the **FUNK MACHINE** specialty is on Bass Guitar. The **FREQUENCY SHIFT** control when used by itself for Bass Guitar will lower the bass response of any amp by at lease two full octaves. When used with the **FILTER RANGE** control the Wa Wa effect comes through with unbelievable bottom, even on the open "E".

The electronics are encased in a strong cast aluminum case trimmed with a silvered face plate, accented by beautiful multi-colored graphics. The footswitch on the unit is an in-out switch which bypasses the electronics when the unit is not in use.

Dimensions 4" wide 5" long 2" high.
Weight 1.75 lbs., Battery included.

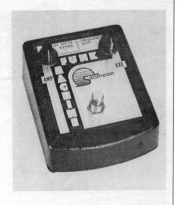

FRESH FUZZ

This "STATE OF THE ART" pre-amp can make a big clean amp sound small and dirty at very low volume levels. It is very much **unlike** fuzz tones that are currently available. Its design makes it possible for a player to play chords as well as single notes.

The word "Fuzz Tone" to most professional guitar players is synonymous with a device that beginning guitar players use to cover up horrendous playing, not so with the **Fresh Fuzz**. It's function is to make over powered amps get that driving **English Rock** sound at small room and small club volumes.

The Fresh Fuzz also may be used as a pre-amp booster by adjusting the attack and gain levels. Using the Fresh Fuzz in this way can take a small amp and give it more **clean** volume.

RETAIL $45.00

BURGESS BATTERY INCLUDED

SEAMOON   2802 TENTH STREET   BERKELEY, CA 94710   PHONE (415) 549-1857

Fresh Fuzz promo.

The FINAL PHASE utilizes a new circuit design to achieve advanced performance at a reasonable price. In addition to nine stages generating over 1600 degrees of phase shift, the FINAL PHASE incorporates several unique features unavailable in any other product.

1. The input signal is amplified through a low-noise FET buffer, whose high input impedence (1 million ohms) provides a negligible load to the guitar pick ups, resulting in clear, undamped high frequency response.

2. In the absence of an input signal, a built in noise gate silently bypasses the phase shift circuits.

3. All controls are compensated to avoid volume changes and undesireable effects, making for easier operation.

4. The exclusive "sweep modulation" circuitry produces effects ranging from an erie warble to abrupt, asymmetrical sweep patterns.

5. Phasing intensity is adjustable with the regenerative feedback control.

6. Extremely low current drain (less than 4 milliamps) insures long battery life. 9 Volt batteries are useful down to 5 Volts.

All JXL products are fully guaranteed for one year of service.

(JXL)

"Final Phase" was an appropriate name for short-lived JXL.

Craig Anderton's Story

In 1967 I published an article in Popular Electronics about building a compressor. I'd previously shown the idea to several companies, but they looked at me like I was from Mars. They couldn't understand why you'd want to make your guitar sound like that. Later I started designing things for a number of companies, one of which was Seamoon. I designed their Funk Machine, an opto-isolator voltage-controlled envelope follower. John Lang made a deal that he would put the things out, take them to NAMM shows, that kind of stuff. This was around 1974. The pedals were well received except for the fact that the plastic cases would break if you stomped on them too hard. The plastic was supposed to be "indestructible," but there's no such thing when you're talking about musicians. Steve Cropper and Larry Graham [Sly Stone's bassist] both bought Funk Machines, and one of Seamoon's employees was Martha Davis, who later became the Motels' singer. I remember her doing the testing by running her fingers over the boards while listening to the sounds. It was an interesting test procedure.

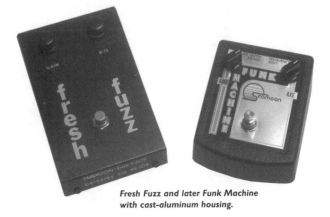

Fresh Fuzz and later Funk Machine with cast-aluminum housing.

135

SOLA COLORSOUND

The mighty Colorsound Overdriver.

Colorsound pedals livened up many an accessories counter in their heyday with their brightly painted contoured-metal cases and flashy graphics. Sola got its start in 1965 at a London music store called Macari's Musical Exchange, on 22 Denmark Street. Owned by brothers Larry and Joe Macari, the store was a popular hangout for such local heavies as Jimmy Page, Jeff Beck, and Pete Townshend.

According to Larry's son Steve Macari, the Colorsound Tone Bender MK I (which differed from the original Vox Tone Bender) was designed at Macari's in '65 by a tech named Gary Hurst. It featured a pressed-steel case and pointer-style knobs for volume and fuzz intensity. Responding to a demand for Tone Benders in mid-'60s

Britain, Sola introduced the Tone Bender Professional MK II, which sported a die-cast alloy case and sold for about £12. Macari ads touted its use by Jeff Beck, the Troggs, Spencer Davis, and the Koobas.

Sola also made pedals for Vox and Marshall. Marshall's Fuzz Unit and the Park Fuzz (a brand name Marshall used in the '70s) looked quite similar to Sola's offerings of the era, as did the Vox Phazer, Wah Swell, Wah Wah, and the three-knob Tone Bender.

Encouraged by their success in the British stomp-box market, the Macari brothers decided to produce pedals under the name Colorsound, with different hues for each effect. By '72 the Colorsound line included the Wah Wah, Dopplatone,

Colorsound Wah-Wah, Tone Bender Jumbo, and Wah-Fuzz.

Cool colors, cool sounds.

Ring Modulator, Octivider, Wah-Fuzz-Swell, Overdriver, Sustain, and Tone Bender. In '74 Sola Sound moved to a larger facility at 165 Burnt Oak Broadway, Edgeware, Middlesex. The Tone Bender was replaced by the Jumbo Tone Bender, which featured a wider case and blue instead of orange lettering. This same case would also house the circa-'77 Supa Tone Bender, which boasted updated circuitry.

By that time Colorsound's offerings included the Tremolo, Overdriver, Octivider, Vocalizer, Wah-Wah, Supa Tone Bender, Flanger, Chuck-A-Wah, V.C.F. (voltage-controlled filter), Wah-Fuzz, Wah-Fuzz-Swell, Wah-Wah Supremo, Jumbo Tonebender, Supa Sustain, Dipthonizer, Ring Modulator, Wah-Swell, Organ Wah-Swell, Phazex, Electro Echo, and Fuzzphase. The company also made guitar amps, P.A. gear, mixers, electric pianos, and pickups.

Colorsound's production officially ceased in the early '80s, but the Macaris—who now owned seven music stores—plus sons Anthony and Steve and their old friend Dick Denney continued producing the Wah-Wah throughout the decade, adding the Wah-Fuzz in 1989. Sola has since reissued a number of their classic boxes, including the MK II and MK III Tone Benders, Tremolo, Octivider, Ring Modulator, Power Boost, Fuzzphase, Wah-Wah, and Wah-Fuzz.

The Sola-made Park Fuzz and Marshall Supa Fuzz.

TUBE WORKS

Guitarists have long been partial to tubes, so why not put one in a stompbox? That's not precisely the question keyboardist and electronics tinkerer Brent Butler pondered in 1978, but since that time, the Tube Driver distortion pedal has attained must-have status among many players. In 1980 Brent started Audio Matrix in Escondido, California, and began making Mini Boogee overdrive preamps. Eric Johnson began praising Butler's creations early in his career. "I use Audio Matrix Mini Boogee tube fuzztones; these sound real great through Marshalls and Twins," Eric told *Guitar Player* in December '82.

Denver, Colorado-based Tube Works is now one of the world's leading manufacturers of tube-powered distortion pedals, rackmount preamps, direct boxes, and reverbs. The company also makes solid-state power amps and hybrid guitar and bass amplifiers that feature Butler's patented MosValve technology.

Brent Butler's Story

I'm not a guitar player. However much I appreciate that talent, my interests have always been in keyboard, which I started playing at age three. In 1968, when I was a teenager, I traded my first motorcycle for a Farfisa Mini Compact organ. The sound of a Hammond B-3 through a wide-open Leslie 147 was about the closest thing to heaven I knew at that time, and in the early '70s Deep Purple's *Book of Taliesyn* and *Made in Japan* piqued my obsession with getting that ominous Hammond growl. Lacking the funds to buy a real Hammond and a Leslie, I was forced to improvise. My dad had an old tube Westinghouse stereo with a high-gain preamp for the ceramic phono cartridge. One day I plugged my Farfisa directly into that input, and suddenly I had the overdrive sound I'd been searching for.

By this time I had also gained a working knowledge of electronics—primarily by blowing up lots of old radios and TVs. After mounting the Westinghouse guts in a box I'd gotten from Radio Shack, the first Tube Driver was born. I used it onstage with two homemade Leslies for several years, and in the meantime I found an old 1939 Hammond model B. Life was good.

One day in '77, a friend of mine named Mark Stoddard was playing his guitar through my stereo Tube Driver. He started freaking out over its over-drive sound and asked if I would make him a single-channel Tube Driver with a master volume to use with his Fender Twin. The unit I made for him was the first guitar Tube Driver. I still have the negative for the circuit board that I laid out for it, dated March 7, 1978. "Butronics" was the name I chose to launch my career.

Circa '79 Tube Driver.

In November 1979 I ran an ad in *Guitar Player* for the Tube Driver model 201. It featured a single-stage 6AV6 tube and a compressor simi-lar to an old MXR Dynacomp for even more sustain. I sold enough units to pay for the ad and a bit more. There was a new-product release in December '79 as well.

Originally called the Mini Boogee, this butler made box was renamed Mini Matrix after protest by Mesa/ Boogie.

At the time I was also designing PC boards and doing tech work for Carvin in Escondido, California. I left Carvin in 1980 and started Audio Matrix in a building Carvin formerly occupied on Industrial Avenue. I continued the Tube Driver theme with a device called the Mini Boogee, which I later renamed Mini Matrix at the strong request of Mesa/Boogie's Randy Smith. That's when I learned about trademarks.

After Audio Matrix folded in '82, I went to work for Dean Markley. Over the next few years I sold a number of old 201s and Mini Matrix units from my home out of the remaining stock. Eric Johnson was an early purchaser of the Mini Matrix. At one time he used six of them—one for each string.

In 1985 Markley and I parted ways, and Paul Chandler started marketing the new updated Tube Driver. I remember baking the silk-screened paint on the first 100 units in my kitchen oven. Then came the Eric Johnson feature in *Guitar Player.* The Chandler Tube Driver was listed as part of his effects chain, and this had a dramatic effect on their demand. I hand-built all of Eric's Tube Drivers, including several with custom bias controls.

My basement was converted into a production area, and 20-hour days were common. But I was on my own and doing what I liked. I built all the Chandler units with the inscription "Concept and design: BK Butler." Tube Drivers that don't have this were made by Chandler without my consent.

In 1989, my company—now called Keynote Industries—started selling the Real Tube pedals. Later, a lower-cost version of the Tube Driver was developed, and I was awarded a U.S. patent for the use of a 9-volt adapter with a tube designed to run on 250 volts. At that time we put the four-knob Tube Driver aside in lieu of the 9-volt model and the new blue and black Real Tube units, which featured electronic switching and more refined tonality. Due to popular demand, we decided to reissue the original Tube Driver in 1995 on a limited basis. The U.S. version of the Ibanez Tube King is also currently being manufactured by Tube Works.

A top choice of Eric Johnson, the Tube Driver's fat distortion came from a 12AX7 preamp tube.

141

TYCHOBRAHE

One of the most enigmatic outfits to jump into the stompbox fray was a Southern California sound-reinforcement company called Tychobrahe. Founded in 1969 by college student Bob Bogdanovich (brother of film director Peter Bogdanovich), Tychobrahe grew rapidly from a small-time P.A. provider to the sound company for some of the '70's biggest acts. Chief engineer Jim Gamble oversaw the design and production of Tychobrahe's mixers, power amps, and speaker systems, as well as their three short-lived pedal offerings—the Octavia, Pedalflanger, and Parapedal wah-wah. Gamble currently heads Gamble and Associates, a California manufacturer of digitally controlled mixers.

The Tychobrahe Octavia was a copy of Roger Mayer's renowned octave fuzz.

Jeff Beck praised the Pedalflanger in a 1980 *Guitar Player* interview: "They only made a few, and I've two of the only ones left. They're amazing." Robin Trower preferred the Parapedal. "To me the wah-wah's a climactic thing," Robin told *Guitar Player* in 1980. "That's the way I use it onstage. When you want to take the song to its highest point, that's where the effect comes in. It makes the guitar sound more aggressive." Who could argue with that?

Jim Gamble's Story

I grew up in Southern California and started doing sound at surfer gigs back in 1958. I had an old Hudson with a huge backseat, and I could put two of my home-built speakers in there. We didn't do the P.A. for the band; we just played records when they stopped. We'd make enough money to go eat afterwards. At that time bands were still plugging their high-impedance mikes into their guitar amps. When Dick Dale came along, he told me, "I want to sing through your shit because it sounds better than *my* shit." We tried it, and he blew all of my speakers. I realized then that this business was harder than I'd thought.

I went to college back when they taught tube theory—a lot of good that did me. I took so many fuckin' math and slide-rule courses it was ridiculous. I joined the Navy in the mid '60s, and they sent me to electronics school.

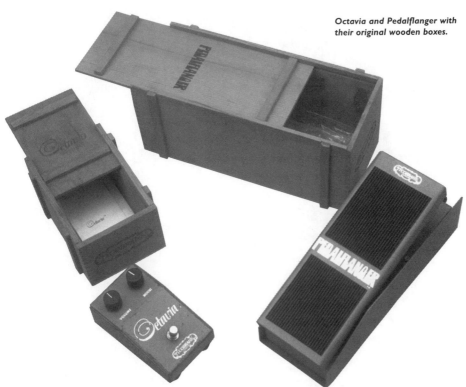

After I got out, I went back to college again. I also played bass in a couple of famous bands that I won't mention. I was doing the club circuit until one day I realized that I wasn't going to make any money at it. I thought, "I'm going to have a lousy, shitty life because I ain't that good."

I started my sound business right then in '69. That's when Bob Bogdanovich came along. Bob was a college kid who just stumbled into the audio business. His father was really rich. He owned Star Kist Tuna and half of the Heinz corporation. Bob got some money from his dad and gave it to the promoters for Civic Presentations, who were putting on a gig at the Rose Bowl. They had done a bunch of other gigs and made lots of money, but this time it rained and nobody came.

They lost their shirts. The only thing they had left was the P.A system that they'd bought from the Beach Boys.

They gave the P.A. to Bob, who just put it in his garage for a couple of months. Then the weather got nice and people started saying, "Hey, break that shit out and let's have a party up at Griffith Park." So Bob started doing free shows there for all the big bands. Pretty soon they started hiring him. I had my own sound company, and I was soon bidding against him for shows around the area. One day we did a Frank Zappa show at Exposition Hall, and we put both systems together. Bob liked the sound and suggested we keep it that way. I thought, "Great, there go all my new mikes."

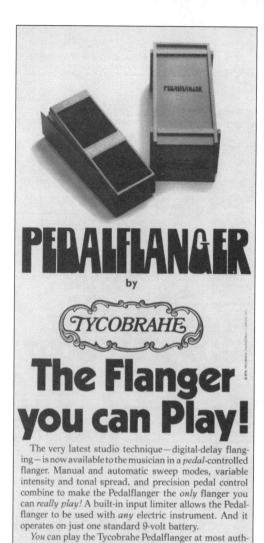
That's how it happened—we just kind of joined up. Later, a couple of other crazy fuckers got involved. They went around stuffing cocaine up everybody's noses to get gigs, and we started gigging. Bob got the name Tychobrahe from the Danish astronomer who was wrong about everything. Tycho Brahe thought the planets revolved around the earth, and he had a gold nose because his had been bitten off. He died of a burst bladder while waiting for the queen to greet him.[1] It was the perfect name for Bob's company. The swirly logo that went around the name came from a mortuary ad that he saw on a bus stop bench.

We started making amps and speakers and mixers back when nothing was any good. It was all Altec tube shit. We built transistor power amps even before Crown. We were doing sound for everybody—Fleetwood Mac, Black Sabbath, Rod Stewart, the Stones. I had to go out on three Stones tours, and I hated it. They're horrible sounding live. Mick put on a great performance, but he sure was a cheap shit. We did a free Stones concert for Bangladesh or some place that was starving to death. We worked out the details, but Mick didn't want to pay us anything.

Bob started going to trade shows, and he liked it. I thought, "God, this is gross." Then he started talking about having a *real* business, and I went, "Listen, there is no real business in *this* business, buddy." He said, "Our consoles aren't selling too good. Can't we make something else that sells a lot?" He wanted pedals, so I said,

1. Brahe (1546-1601) actually made some of the most accurate astronomical observations of the pre-telescope era. But because he was unable to detect annual variation in the relative directions of the stars—which, he correctly assumed, should be visible if the Earth revolves around the sun—he rejected the Copernican system and believed that the sun revolves around the earth. Johann Kepler used Brahe's observations in deducing his laws of planetary motion.

A mint-condition Pedalflanger.

"Okay, we'll make them, but don't chew *me* out when it doesn't work out. He told me that if I just whipped some out, he'd send me to Hawaii for a vacation. So I said okay.

For a while it was quite a scene. Bob had a whole production line set up, and he brought in a bunch of Vietnamese solder chicks. The Octavia came about after Noel Redding brought in an original Roger Mayer Octavia that was broken. After I fixed it, he asked if I could copy it. Everybody went, "Oh, you copied it—now let's make a million of them!" That's what started it. Bucket-brigade technology had just come along, so I told them we could make a delay that could also do flanging. That turned into the Pedalflanger. It was a cheesy piece of shit because it had to be so cheap, but it was still highly technical. It needed a compressor to keep from clipping the fucking bucket brigade, noise reduction, gates, and this and that.

Then they wanted another pedal, so I said, "Well, how about a wah-wah?" It seemed like the natural choice. Let's see, you've got your distortion box, your flanger, and your wah-wah pedal. So we made the Parapedal. It was a little different, though, because when you pushed back on the heel it would go real low.

For the boxes we picked some metal shop that did steel only. I told them it was stupid and that we should be making them out of aluminum. They went, "No, no, that's too expensive," and I'm thinking, "You guys are fucked." The fuckin' things weighed so much it cost a million dollars to ship them anywhere. I reluctantly made the pedals, but it wasn't my forte. Tychobrahe sold hundreds of them, but they never made any money at it. Around '77 we a did a big festival with zillions of people and I went, "This is enough—I'm starting my own company."

The Parapedal was Tychobrahe's answer to the CryBaby Wah.

145

UNIVOX

Univox was a brand name used by New York's Merson Musical Products company, a big-time guitar distributor since the '40s. Merson was purchased by Gulf+Western in the mid-'60s, which then changed the name to Unicord. Unicord distributed Marshall and Korg products in the U.S. until 1985, when it was taken over by Korg.

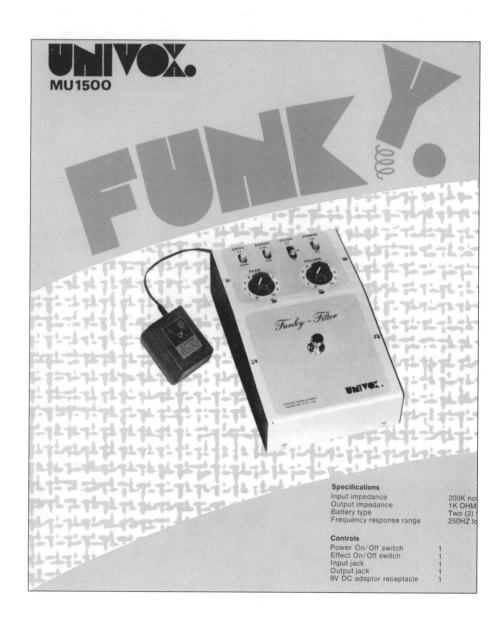

UNIVOX.
MU1500

FUNK!

Funky - Filter

UNIVOX.

Specifications

Input impedance	200K no
Output impedance	1K OHM
Battery type	Two (2)
Frequency response range	250HZ to

Controls

Power On/Off switch	1
Effect On/Off switch	1
Input jack	1
Output jack	1
9V DC adaptor receptacle	1

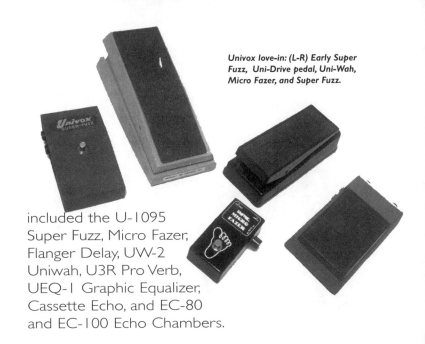

Univox love-in: (L-R) Early Super Fuzz, Uni-Drive pedal, Uni-Wah, Micro Fazer, and Super Fuzz.

Univox never made any effects. They simply determined what was needed for their accessories line and subcontracted the work to Japanese electronics companies such as Shin-Ei. By the mid '70s Univox's offerings included the U-1095 Super Fuzz, Micro Fazer, Flanger Delay, UW-2 Uniwah, U3R Pro Verb, UEQ-1 Graphic Equalizer, Cassette Echo, and EC-80 and EC-100 Echo Chambers.

Univox Super Fuzzz U-1095

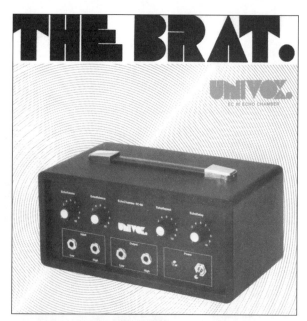

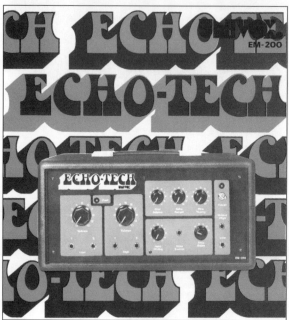

Eddie Van Halen's early setup featured an unspecified Univox echo that he stashed inside a World War II practice bomb. "I had a different motor put in it so it would delay much slower and go really low," he told *Guitar Player*. "I use this for 'Eruption'."

One of Univox's biggest hits was the Uni-Vibe, a compact phaser/vibrato originally developed to simulate a rotating speaker for keyboards. Designed by Shin-Ei engineer Fumio Mieda, the Uni-Vibe used a pulsating light source and four photo resistors to modulate its four-stage phase-shifting circuit up to 720 degrees. Primitive technology for sure, but its thick, smoky phase sound is still unique and cool.

The Phazer's "Univox" video counter pulses in time with rate control settings.

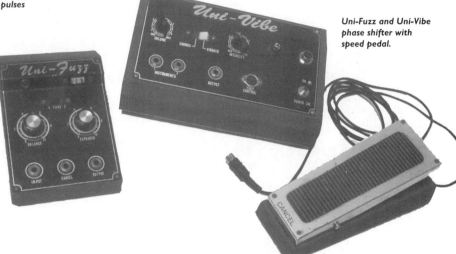

Uni-Fuzz and Uni-Vibe phase shifter with speed pedal.

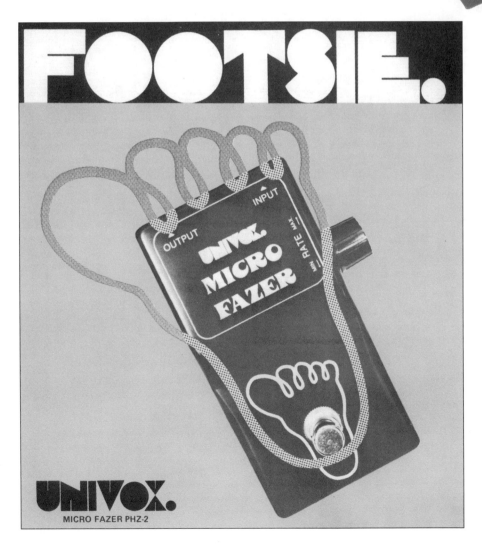

UNIVOX.
UEQ-1 Graphic Equalizer
List $225.00T.

BAND·AID.

Univox introduced the Uni-Vibe into the U.S. in 1969 as the U-915 Shiftee Uni-Vibe, and it was also offered in the Lafayette Electronics catalog as the Roto-Vibe, other manifestations of this famous effect include the Jax Vibra-Chorus (with "psychedelic mood adjuster" control) and Guild's Rotoverb. Jimi Hendrix made the Uni-Vibe famous, using it to crank up the psychedelia quotient on songs such as "Little Wing," "Voodoo Chile," "The Wind Cries Mary," and "Are You Experienced?" Robin Trower was another major fan of the Uni's sweet swirl. New versions of the Uni-Vibe are offered by companies such as Jim Dunlop (who owns the rights to the name), Prescription Electronics, VooDoo Lab, Custom Audio, and Fulltone.

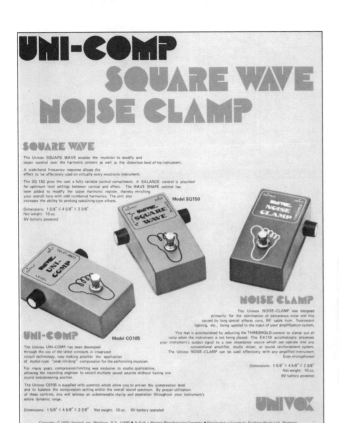

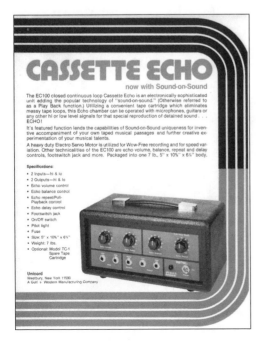

One of the largest and most successful musical instrument companies of the mid '60s was Vox, maker of such British Invasion standards as the Phantom series guitars and the AC15, AC30, and AC100 (Super Beatle) amplifiers. Vox was also one of the first with an extensive accessories line, which began with the Vibravox vibrato/ "tremulant" device and grew to include distortion units, tape echoes, and even a wireless microphone—a cutting-edge concept in 1964. In conjunction with their American partner, Thomas Organ, Vox introduced many effects, including the Tone Bender Fuzz and Tone Bender MK III (the latter resembled the like-named Colorsound unit), the Clyde McCoy and CryBaby wah-wah pedals, the Wow Swell (a combination volume and wah-wah pedal), Wow Fuzz (wah-wah/fuzz pedal), Stereo Fuzz-Wah (reportedly designed by Jose Arrondondo), Repeat Percussion, V8161 Deluxe Distortion Booster, V840 Treble Bass Booster, Super Phase, Power Booster and Distortion Booster (each sported one knob and was roughly the size and shape of an MXR Phase 90), V807 Echo Reverb, V829 Percussion King, V837 Echo Deluxe, and V815 Bandmaster.

In the early '80s Vox came out with a series of stompboxes that were simply labeled Wah, Compressor, Flanger, Distortion, Phaser, and Chorus.

Early '60s Vox promo shows the Vibravox vibrato and tremulant unit.

Vox founder Tom Jennings was an accordion player and organist who opened a music store in Dartford, Kent, after World War II. With the help of electronics engineer Derek Underdown, Jennings started building electronic organs and other electric instruments under the name Jennings Organ Company. In 1956 Jennings heard an amp built by a guitarist and electronics tech named Dick Denney. Jennings and Denney had worked in the same Vickers armament plant during the war, and had often played music together during the hours spent in the factory's underground air-raid shelter. Impressed by Denney's creation, Jennings hired him as a technician for what was now called Jennings Musical Industries.

Vox Tone Benders

153

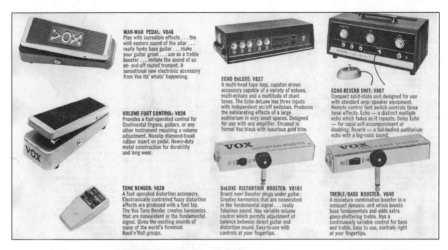

JMI's first guitar amp, the Vox AC15, was introduced in 1958. The AC30 followed in '59 and was soon being used by such top groups as the Shadows and the Beatles. The Beatles' explosive popularity soon created a demand that outstripped JMI's production capabilities, so Jennings entered into a licensing agreement with Thomas Organ. Jennings also needed to raise capital to expand JMI's facilities, so in '64 he sold Vox to Britain's Royston Group. Vox was sold to Dallas-Arbiter in '69 and later to Marshall.

After selling Vox, Jennings and Denney started Jennings Electronic Developments, which made a wah/volume pedal, and a couple of unique devices known as the Bushwacker and the Cyclone. JED also introduced a series of effects that featured a foot-actuated rotary control instead of a pedal, including the Growler (wah/fuzz), Repeater, Fuzz, Wah-Wah, Hi-Lo Boost, Harmonic Boost, Siren Foot Control (wah, fuzz, and siren effects), and the Scrambler, a large triangular unit that featured dual rotary controls— one for volume/intensity, one for wah.

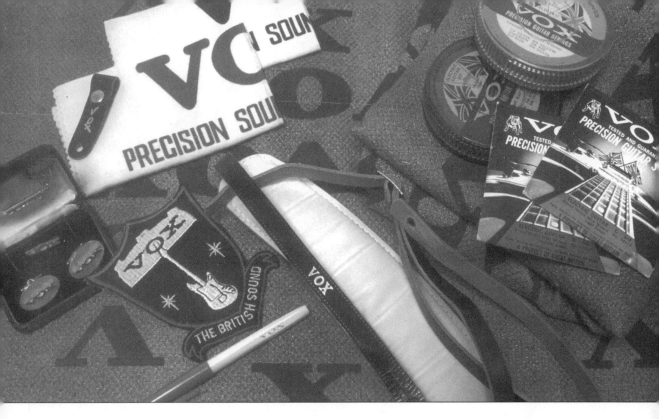

Vox currently makes the V829 Tone Bender and V847 Wah-Wah. Jim Dunlop offers the CryBaby, Bass CryBaby, CryBaby Octave Wah, and Mister CryBaby Super Volume Pedal. Tom Jennings died in 1978.

Dick Denney's Story

When I went to Thomas Organ in Sepulveda, California, in '65 to check on how our products were being made—the AC30, in particular—they told me about [trumpeter] Clyde McCoy. That's where they got the name for their wah-wah, which they were in the process of testing. [Thomas Organ president] Joe Benaron's team had developed a very good solid-state amplifier [the Super Beatle] that had a 3-position midrange-boost voicing switch. I was quite impressed with it.

In England we had the solid-state T60 amps, which used the old germanium transistors, but America's silicon technology was more advanced—especially on the music side.

There was a brilliant chap in the lab named Brad Plunkett. He invented the wah-wah. Since we were two Vox companies, whatever we did we gave to them, and vice versa. They brought the wah-wah over to London on a little tag board, and I was the first one in England to demo the damn thing. We did it at ITV studios in Kingsway for a show called *Town and Around*. It caused such a stir that we had to lock it away. Then we took it to the Frankfurt trade show. Everyone was after it, and because Thomas Organ hadn't brought a patent out on it, we had to lock it in the hotel safe until I was ready to use it.

Doo-dads deluxe: Vox strings, strap, cufflinks, jacket emblem, pen, key fob, banners and, underneath it all, curtains!

Vox sampler: (L-R) Early Thomas Organ CryBaby, Fuzz Wah Volume, Tone Benders, V-847 Wah Wah, Treble Bass Booster, Repeat Percussion, and Treble Bass Booster boxes, King Wah.

When we had to start making the wah-wahs in England, my idea was to encapsulate them in epoxy. That was a bit of a mistake. The Italian company EMI—which was part of EKO guitars—started building them for Thomas, and that's where the circuit got out. I'm afraid Thomas lost out on that because they hadn't gotten a patent. There weren't very many made at Jennings in Dartford. We had to get some going, though, and since we couldn't wait for the Italians, my wife Dolly and I would build them in a little shed in our garden. In '68 the CryBaby came out, which had a shorter pedal travel. Then the Italians started to ship them to England under the name of Jen. After that, everyone started making wah-wahs.

Rare '70s Vox catalog pages with Colorsound-built Tone Bender.

VOX ACCESSORIES

Vox guitarstrings

Vox Guitar Strings are available in wallets of six or twelve, or as single-string individual packets.

Six-String Sets. Ultra light gauge; round wound nickel; light gauge; light gauge chrome; round wound nickel; medium gauge; nylon wound with first and second strings plain; medium tape wound; silver plated nylon spanish.

Twelve-String Sets. Round wound twelve-string; tape wound twelve-string.

Bass String Sets. Chrome tape wound bass; nylon tape wound bass. String your sound on Vox!

Tonebender MkIII

Acts as a volume control with foot switch-operated fuzz. Bring in the fuzz and control the volume you need in the normal way.

Switch-off in normal Vox foot pedal style when it's time to ditch the fuzz. Fit between instrument and amp as a straight volume regulator.

Wow Fuzz

Wah-Wah pedal with a great new fuzzy sound built into it. Play it as a straight Wah-Wah – then a tap of the toe phases in the fuzz. Wah-Wah PLUS fuzz! The new knock-out sound that will have them up in arms.

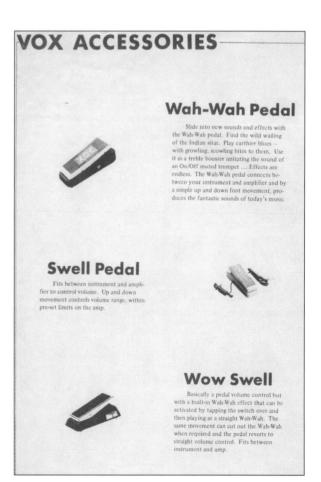

VOX ACCESSORIES

Wah-Wah Pedal

Slide into new sounds and effects with the Wah-Wah pedal. Find the wild wailing of the Indian sitar. Play earthier blues – with growling, scowling bites to them. Use it as a treble booster imitating the sound of an On/Off muted trumpet ....Effects are endless. The Wah-Wah pedal connects between your instrument and amplifier and by a simple up and down foot movement, produces the fantastic sounds of today's music.

Swell Pedal

Fits between instrument and amplifier to control volume. Up and down movement controls volume range, within pre-set limits on the amp.

Wow Swell

Basically a pedal volume control but with a built-in Wah-Wah effect that can be activated by tapping the switch over and then playing as a straight Wah-Wah. The same movement can cut out the Wah-Wah when required and the pedal reverts to straight volume control. Fits between instrument and amp.

Sometimes the truth hurts.

Around '60 or '61 we'd gotten an overdrive that probably came from the U.S. It was rather horrible sounding, but you could almost get a saxophone sound out of it that I quite liked. Tom used to tell people we were trying to get rid of distortion, but I *loved* it. He knew the market was there, though, so we began to make our own distortion box, which we called the Tone Bender. When the Rolling Stones began using fuzz, everyone started buying Tone Benders. Our first unit was just a little square box with a jack on it that you plugged into your guitar. I didn't like that. We also had a treble booster and a bass booster in the same box. All we had at that time were the little black Mullard OC77 germanium transistors. I think that's where we got our sound, though, because when we later tried silicon transistors, we couldn't get it. If you want that deep, concrete-grinding sound, you've got to use germanium. You can get an equivalent germanium transistor today, but it just isn't the same.

VOX ACCESSORIES

Distortion Booster

Tone-distortion comes easy when you fit this small battery powered unit into your jack-plug socket. A jack lead connects the booster unit to the amp. Distortion is brought into play by an On/Off switch on the booster pack, and two controls vary — 1 volume; 2 distortion sustain. Disconnect from amp to obtain maximum hours from battery when not in use.

Repeater Percussion

Similar to the Distortion Unit and connects the same way. On/Off switch brings it into use, and each chord played on the instrument is a repeated pulsating beat. Rate of repeat can be varied from the rotary control on the repeater. Battery operated.

Treble/Bass Booster

A tone control unit that plugs into your instrument and connects by lead to the amp. With instrument and amp preset to desired limits, the booster is switched on and off with its own switch, and a rotary control covers treble/bass boost. A wide range of tones from very high treble to super-deep bass is the result of this new innovation.

Multi Plug Board

All rubber solid construction, fused for safety. The plug board can run four separate amplifiers from the mains. It is invaluable to all groups and is manufactured to Vox specifications.

157

Vox Effects Pedals

Vox's Dallas-Arbiter-era effects comeback.

A friend of ours named Larry Macari [of Sola/Colorsound] used to make pedals for us in the old days. Actually, most of the work was done by a guy named Doug McDonnel. Colorsound even came out with their own Tone Bender after Vox. They really worked on it, and it sounded very good.

When Meazzi tape echoes started coming into England from Italy in 1958, Tom asked me to see what I thought of them. I liked them quite a lot, so we decided to start making our own tape echoes. The first was called the Vox Echo. It was modeled on the Meazzi system, but it had a better drive mechanism. Next came the three-head and later the six-head Shadows Echo, which got a proper motor like you'd find in a good tape recorder, so that it would be nice and stable. We kept working on the echoes for quite a number of years, but we left it to another chap to build them for us. We made many of the pedals at Vox, but we also used subcontractors.

The Clyde McCoy evolution.

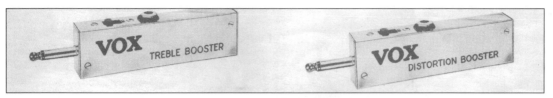

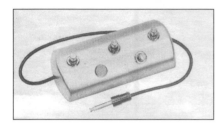

Partial effects lineup for 1966.

When I went to Thomas Organ in '65, Stan Cutler showed me their latest echo technology. He took me into this area where you had to wear a special suit to protect you from the electrolyte solution that they used to coat these cylinders that looked like treacle tins. The cylinders were then filled with another kind of electrolyte. When the drum was turned by an electric motor, it worked like a variable capacitor that could store a charge for a certain amount of time. It worked all right, but they never really perfected it. All the Vox tape echoes were made in England, but by '67 Tom and I were both gone from the company, so I don't know what happened with the Thomas echo after that. We had a lot of young people working in our lab, and some of them would knock off our circuits. I think that's why a lot of our early designs such as the fuzz were leaked out.

After Vox, Tom and I started up a little business called Jennings Electronic Developments. We came out with a wah/volume pedal that had a platform [rocker] that went from right to left. I also developed a thing called the Bushwacker, which was a very early synthesizer. It had several sounds on it—more like croaks, really. It was very odd. Another was the Cyclone, which gave you hurricane sounds when you moved the pedal from right to left.

In '82 Larry Macari asked if I could build them a new wah-wah. I revisited a circuit I'd come up with years before that didn't use an inductor. We started off with 25 units, and we're still making them today.

When it comes to guitars, we wrote the book

The Ukulele
A Visual History • Jim Beloff

The humble ukulele has left its mark on popular music and culture not only in Hawaii but throughout the world. This book provides a colorful look at the past and present of this intriguing, diminutive musical instrument. It's packed with photos of rare and unusual ukuleles, and memorabilia such as whimsical sheet music covers and witty advertisements.

Softcover, 112pp, 200 color photos, 7-3/8 x 9-1/4, ISBN 0-87930-454-5, $24.95

Secrets from the Masters
40 Great Guitar Players
Edited by Don Menn

Featuring the most influential guitarists of the past 25 years: Jimi Hendrix, Les Paul, Eric Clapton, Eddie Van Halen, Chuck Berry, Andrés Segovia, Pete Townshend and more. Combines personal biography, career history, and playing techniques.

Softcover, 300 pp, 8-1/2 x 11, ISBN 0-87930-260-7, $19.95

Blues Guitar • The Men Who Made the Music
Second Edition • Edited by Jas Obrecht

Readers get a look inside the lives and music of thirty great bluesmen, through interviews, articles, discographies, and rare photographs. Covers Buddy Guy, Robert Johnson, John Lee Hooker, Albert King, B.B. King, Muddy Waters, and more.

Softcover, 280pp, 8-1/2 x 11, ISBN 0-87930-292-5, $22.95

Bass Heroes
Styles, Stories & Secrets of 30 Great Bass Players • Edited by Tom Mulhern

Thirty of the world's greatest bass players in rock, jazz, studio/pop, and blues & funk share their musical influences, playing techniques, and opinions. Includes Jack Bruce, Stanley Clarke, James Jamerson, Paul McCartney, and more.

Softcover, 208pp, 8-1/2 x 11, ISBN 0-87930-274-7, $19.95

The Fender Amp Book
A Complete History of Fender Amplifiers
By John Morrish

Before Fender electric guitars became household words, Fender amplifiers were already making the scene. Here is the absorbing tale of how Fender fame spread via one of the company's most important product lines.
Hardcover, 96pp, 4-1/2 x 9-1/8, ISBN 0-87930-345-X, $17.95

How to Play Guitar
The Basics & Beyond–Chords, Scales, Tunes & Tips
By the Editors of Guitar Player

For anyone learning to play acoustic or electric guitar, this book and CD set is packed with music, licks, and lessons from the pros. The CD guides readers through nine lessons. *Softcover, 80 pp, 8-1/2 x 11, ISBN 0-87930-399-9, $14.95*

Hot Guitar
Rock Soloing, Blues Power, Rapid-Fire Rockabilly, Slick Turnarounds, and Cool Licks • By Arlen Roth

This collection of hot techniques and cool licks includes detailed instruction and hundreds of musical examples. This book covers string bending, slides, picking and fingering techniques, soloing, and rock, blues, and country licks.

Softcover, 160pp, 8-1/2 x 11, ISBN 0-87930-276-3, $19.95

Picks! The Colorful Saga of Vintage Celluloid Guitar Plectrums • By Will Hoover

An eye-catching look back at the vast variety and fascinating history of vintage celluloid guitar picks. "Will Hoover has taken what you might imagine to be a mundane subject and made it fascinating." —*Billboard*
Softcover, 107pp, 6-1/2 x 6-1/2, ISBN 0-87930-377-8, $12.95

Jaco • The Extraordinary and Tragic Life of Jaco Pastorius, "The World's Greatest Bass Player"
By Bill Milkowski

This is a fitting tribute to the talented but tormented genius who revolutionized the electric bass and single-handedly fused jazz, classical, R&B, rock, reggae, pop, and punk—all before the age of 35, when he met his tragic death.

Hardcover, 264pp, 6 x 9, ISBN 0-87930-361-1, $22.95

Guitar Player Repair Guide
How to Set Up, Maintain, and Repair Electrics and Acoustics
By Dan Erlewine—Second Edition

Whether you're a player, collector, or repairperson, this hands-on guide provides all the essential information on caring for guitars and electric basses. Includes hundreds of photos and drawings detailing techniques for guitar care and repair.

Softcover, 309pp, 8-1/2 x 11, ISBN 0-87930-291-7, $22.95

Do-It-Yourself Projects for Guitarists
35 Useful, Inexpensive Electronic Projects to Help Unlock Your Instrument's Potential
By Craig Anderton

A step-by-step guide for electric guitarists who want to create maximum personalized sound with minimum electronic problems, and get the satisfaction of achieving all this themselves.

Softcover, 176pp, 7-3/8 x 10-7/8, ISBN 0-87930-359-X, $19.95

The Bass Book
A Complete Illustrated History of Bass Guitars
By Tony Bacon and Barry Moorhouse

Celebrating the electric bass and its revolutionary impact on popular music worldwide, this richly colorful history features rare, classic and modern basses, plus exclusive quotes from Paul McCartney, Stanley Clarke, and other bass greats.

Hardcover, 108pp, 7-1/2 x 9-3/4, ISBN 0-87930-368-9, $22.95

The Chinery Collection
150 Years of American Guitars
by Scott Chinery and Tony Bacon

Scott Chinery's fantastic collection can at last be seen in this beautifully illustrated book, documenting the designs, technology, and art of the greatest guitars of recent times. It tells the full story of the American guitar, from the 1800s to today.

Hardcover & slipcase, 132 pp, 500 color photos, 10 x 12-3/4, ISBN 0-87930-482-0, $75.00

Gibson's Fabulous Flat-Top Guitars
By Eldon Whitford, David Vinopal, and Dan Erlewine

250 photos and detailed text illustrate the development of Gibson's flat-tops, showing why these guitars have been the choice of so many great musicians over the decades. Includes detailed specs on historic and modern Gibson flat-tops.

Softcover, 207pp, 8-1/2 x 11, ISBN 0-87930-297-6, $22.95

The Story of the Fender Stratocaster
"Curves, Contours and Body Horns" — A Celebration of the World's Greatest Guitar
By Ray Minhinnett and Bob Young

This loving profile of the American electric guitar that gave us rock 'n' roll and changed pop culture forever features exclusive interviews and color photos of the legendary Strat, its creators, and famous players.
Hardcover, 128pp, 9-1/6 x 11, ISBN 0-87930-349-2, $24.95

Gibson's Fabulous Flat-Top Guitars
By Eldon Whitford, David Vinopal, and Dan Erlewine

250 photos and detailed text illustrate the development of Gibson's flat-tops, showing why these guitars have been the choice of so many great musicians over the decades. Includes detailed specs on historic and modern Gibson flat-tops.

Softcover, 207pp, 8-1/2 x 11, ISBN 0-87930-297-6, $22.95

Gruhn's Guide to Vintage Guitars
An Identification Guide for American Fretted Instruments
By George Gruhn and Walter Carter

This portable reference for identifying American guitars, mandolins, and basses provides comprehensive dating information and model specifications for nearly 2,000 instruments made by all major U.S. manufacturers.
Hardcover, 384pp, 4 x 7-1/2, ISBN 0-87930-195-3, $22.95

The Art of Inlay • Contemporary Design & Technique
By Larry Robinson

This is a dazzling, full-color celebration of both the magical art of inlay and a hands-on guide to its endless creative potential. Includes 70 photos of exquisitely inlaid guitars, banjos, mandolins and various objets d'art, plus how-to instructions.

Hardcover, 112pp, 7-1/2 x 9-1/2, ISBN 0-87930-332-8, $24.95

Miller Freeman Books

Available at fine book and music stores, or contact:

Miller Freeman Books, 6600 Silacci Way, Gilroy, CA 95020
Phone (800) 848-5594 • Fax (408) 848-5784 • E-Mail: mfbooks@mfi.com
World Wide Web: http://www.books.mfi.com